GETTING BACK THE
LOVE WE HAD

GETTING BACK THE LOVE WE HAD

Forty-Two Answers To Real Questions From Couples
Who Feared They Were Losing Their Way

A TRILOGY

Volume Three
A New Focus On Each Other

Francine Beauvoir, PhD and Bruce Crapuchettes, PhD

With a Foreword
by
Harville Hendrix, PhD and
Helen LaKelly Hunt, PhD

GETTING BACK THE LOVE WE HAD
Forty-Two Answers To Real Questions From Couples Who Feared They Were Losing Their Way
A TRILOGY - Volume Three
A New Focus On Each Other

Library of Congress Cataloging-in-Publication Data

Beauvoir, PhD., Francine C.
Crapuchettes, PhD., Bruce

GETTING BACK THE LOVE WE HAD
Forty-Two Answers To Real Questions From Couples Who Feared They Were Losing Their Way
A TRILOGY - Volume Three
A New Focus On Each Other

ISBN-13: 9781979006279
ISBN-10: 197900627X

Library of Congress Control Number: 2017916659
CreateSpace Independent Publishing Platform
North Charleston, South Carolina

Also by Francine Beauvoir and Bruce Crapuchettes:

GETTING BACK THE LOVE WE HAD
Forty-Two Answers To Real Questions From Couples Who Feared They Were Losing Their Way
A TRILOGY - Volume One
Ending the Power Struggle

GETTING BACK THE LOVE WE HAD
Forty-Two Answers To Real Questions From Couples Who Feared They Were Losing Their Way
A TRILOGY - Volume Two
Rebuilding Our Dream

AN IMAGO CLINICAL HANDBOOK: 300 Questions Answered from 20 Years of Training Psychotherapists in Imago Relationship Therapy

By Francine Beauvoir:
RAISING COOPERATIVE & SELF-CONFIDENT CHILDREN: A Step-by-Step Guide for Conscious Parenting

To Harville and Helen
our mentors and friends

and

to our children:
Jon and wife Monica, Dominic and wife Karen,
Mishka, and Natalie and husband Tim

and

to Sachiye, our very special step-granddaughter

Contents
Volume Three

Hello everyone! Are you ready to continue our conversation to-gether? Or maybe, this is your first book in this series. Regardless, we welcome you.

This volume is the last of a trilogy entitled, *"Getting Back The Love We Had."* While each book belongs to the trilogy, it is also designed to be purchased and read separately.

The emphasis of the first volume is showing you a way to, "End the Power Struggle". We go over the foundation and six pillars of a strong relationship, conditions we see as essential to achieve that goal.

In the second volume, Harville and Helen describe the historical shift from the individual to the relational paradigm, powerfully making the case that we are all connected. We believe that couples interested in what we have to say and therefore having purchased our book have ex-perienced, to some degree, a rupture in their connection, a rupture that left a trail of anger and tears. How do we "touch souls again" and recap-ture the dream we once had? Part of that work, is to develop together a vision of what your dream relationship looks like. Read it to each other regularly in a meditative manner and include thanking each other as part of that ritual (for more detail, see volume two, chapter three).

In this, the last volume, we want to focus our efforts on learning how to keep each other safe. To that end, we have previously recommended couples use a structured way of talking to each other about potentially divisive issues. We believe that this manner of interacting with each other, which we call the "Formal Dialogue", is akin to meditating with one another, not just in each other's presence, but actively focusing on each other. Meditation has well known positive effects on a person. Meditation *with* your partner will have a profound reparative effect on your relationship.

Let's go and explore that path together.

The Acknowledgment, Foreword and Introduction are the same as in volume one and two. If you have read either volume, you may want to go directly to chapter 1.

Acknowledgments

The first person we want to publicly acknowledge is Harville Hendrix. Meeting him has changed the course of our lives as a couple and professionally. He has been our mentor, our guide and our inspiration even in times of discomfort.

We are grateful to his wife, Helen LaKelly Hunt, for her generous sharing, both materially and philosophically. We have spent numerous hours listening to Helen's wonderfully provocative thinking, expressed so clearly. She read this book carefully and gave insightful feedback that was both encouraging and necessary. Harville and Helen have enriched us by the manner in which they seamlessly flow with one another.

We have been powerfully influenced by Dan Siegel's books and trainings. They brought us into an "aha" moment and led to our understanding of the Dialogue as Relational Meditation (see Volume Three).

Our clients hold a special place in the birthing of this book. Their questions provided grist for the mill and "forced us" to continually sharpen our thinking and our skills. They encouraged us to write and publish and they kept us on the journey.

Dan Prosser, a published author, provided us with valuable insights and referred us to his competent editor, Doug McNair, who enhanced the book to a professional level.

Bob Kamm, also a published author, and his psychotherapist wife, Andrea, spent time engaging and fostering us to write more clearly and led us to Jane Friedman. We listened to her 24 lecture course called "How To Publish Your Book". We had been so ignorant and naive about the publishing world. Professor Friedman, thank you.

We thank Karl and Darian. While in Paris, we struck a friendship with a couple - Karl Steinberg and Darian Jofikarsthira. They are brilliant public relations people and live in Sri Lanka. One day in a lovely restaurant near the Chateau de Malmaison (where Napoleon and Josephine lived) we had an intense brain storming session. This led us to the following titles:

GETTING BACK THE LOVE WE HAD
Answers To Real Questions From Couples Who
Feared They Were Losing Their Way
Volume One: *Ending the Power Struggle*
Volume Two: *Rebuilding Our Dream*
Volume Three: *A New Focus On Each Other*

Last but not least, we want to thank our children: Jon, Dominic, Mishka, and Natalie. Without them, we would never have undertaken the personal changes we did. They're the ones who over and over again, not always kindly, but so effectively, brought us to our knees. By grace we listened. Together we are conquering. Dominic, especially, has shown interest and given us valuable feedback – "Bor-r-r-r-ing Dad. Get rid of that whole chapter!!"

Your contributions have made this manuscript what it is today. We thank you all!

With Deep Gratitude,

Francine Beauvoir &
Bruce Crapuchettes

Foreword
by
Harville Hendrix, PhD, and Helen LaKelly Hunt, PhD
New York and Dallas, June 2016

" Getting Back The Love We Had" is a three volume series offering a new way to think about being coupled up. It's also a new way to write a book. We start by telling you something about the authors, our relationship with them, and our appreciation for what they have done.

Francine Beauvoir and Bruce Crapuchettes are a married team. Both are clinical psychologists and senior faculty of the Imago International Institute and have long careers as certified Imago clinicians. In addition to training therapists in Imago Relationship Therapy, they conduct private and group therapy sessions, and lead couples workshops. And now they have become authors.

We have known the authors for several decades — long ago as students who became colleagues in the development of Imago, and who then became very dear friends. They have been ardent advocates of the purity of Imago theory; careful practitioners of Imago processes and their contributions to theory and practice constitute important elements of the Imago corpus. In addition, they have been among the first

Imago instructors to take Imago off shore to Australia, New Zealand and France, contributing to its current residence in about 37 countries.

As friends, we have shared our struggles as couples to integrate developing a conscious relationship into our personal lives, a not so easy task! We especially acknowledge that when we were in the depths of our despair, they were our support, and as we climbed back into the sunlight they celebrated with us. They have been our faithful supporters for nearly three decades, and we are honored to be theirs. We share the confidence that we can recover and grow both from the challenges and the joys of our relationships.

There are several aspects of the book that are special. The first is their creating it as a couple. It is rare to find a book for couples written by a couple, both of whom are credentialed as psychologists and practice couples therapy together. Thus, you can be sure that while they are clinical academics, this book flows with the rawness of their own encounters and from decades of lived experience. It is the vulnerable sharing of their own personal suffering, combined with the breakthroughs they achieved, that will inspire the transformation of your own relationship.

The second special feature of this series is its contribution to Imago theory. They make a bold assertion that both persons in a couple's conflict contribute *equally* to the tension by wanting to be the definer of reality. Identifying this as the source of all conflict, they have laid out, in Volume One, six pillars of a strong relationship:

1) Assume the best of your partner.
2) Assume the best of yourself.
3) Contain: Move away from reactivity.
4) Own your stuff.
5) Speak from a place of vulnerability.

Then in number six they offer the radical and transformative challenge:

6) Expect nothing in return for a gift of love.

We believe as you, the readers, integrate these 6 pillars into your lives, you will feel fortified by their wisdom.

A third special aspect of the book is their identification of the Formal Dialogue as Relational Meditation, joining others who seek to integrate mindfulness and psychotherapy. This insight happened serendipitously in a course they were attending on mindfulness where they had an "aha" experience that mindfulness and dialogue were similar and they had been teaching mindfulness to their clients for decades. But they also saw a distinct difference. Both have a focusing process. But mindfulness is the practice of being present in the moment to ones subjective processes. Dialogue is the practice of being present in the moment to whatever arises in the inter-subjective space. Being mindfully listened to allows and accelerates access to experiences and feelings that have not been put into language before and brings them into consciousness. Mirroring mindfully allows one to suspend their own mental processing and become fully present to their partner. The vulnerability achieved by mindful sharing and mindfully listening increases connection and contributes to the integration of the upper and lower regions of the brains of each partner.

The fourth feature is the method the authors use to share their wisdom. Rather than writing a book filled with discursive chapters illustrated with composite clinical examples, the authors chose to solicit real questions from real couples. This gives voice to the real, everyday questions of actual couples whose struggles and hopes drove them to Bruce and Francine's Q&A blogs and practice. The authors share their relational wisdom with each as a sort of personal consultation. While much of it is shared experience, which adds to its credibility, most of it is clinical which shines light on the depth of their grasp of the inner working of intimate relationships and grasp of Imago therapy. Following the spirit of the dialogical process, which they are teaching, they engage the couples in a dialogue about nearly every subject one can imagine couples experience. Receiving couple's questions weekly for over two years and writing a weekly blog as their answers has expanded the reach of their healing wisdom. The multiplicity and diversity of their answers are fascinating. You the reader will feel like you are walking through a relational Library and/or reading an Encyclopedia of relational wisdom, from which you yourself can select the issues about which you want to become more knowledgeable.

The necessity for this book is obvious if we observe that the divorce rate in the post-war western world began to rise in the 1950's, as a result of the impact of the returning veterans on gender roles in families and reached 50% in the 1970s.

Currently, the highest divorce rate occurs in the seventh year of marriage and the first three years of retirement. What is also tragic is that marital satisfaction research assigns happiness to less than one quarter of intact marriages. And, since the beginning of the 21st century, co-habitation agreements outnumber marriage vows and the birth of children outside of marriage is astronomical.

It is clearly the case that marriage as we know it is obsolete and that we must create a new marital/couplehood narrative. All these factors make the dissemination of the information about healthy intimate relationships in this book essential. We are delighted to be partners with them in the creation of a new kind of intimate relationship.

We love this series. We suggest that you read all 126 Q&As in small bits, savoring each morsel of insight with the confidence that you are absorbing the wisdom of experienced clinical minds and being guided into a world you have never known, but which has always been your dream. Please share them with your friends so the process of relational transformation can spread.

Introduction

The bulk of this series of three books consists of our answers to 126 questions gathered during two and half years of our "Friday's Q&A Blog For Couples". We have broken the questions and answers into three volumes. We start and end each volume with chapters explaining the crucial dynamics of committed couples.

All the questions are asked by real couples and the answers are saturated with principles whose goal is to teach us how to relate to each other as conscious, committed, intimate and equal partners. Each entry consists of one question sent in by a member of a couple followed by our answer. Our answer is to the person who sent the question. The answer is not to the couple. This grounds us in the concept that all couples work is personal work!

While we want to take each other seriously, we also want to laugh and enjoy life together. To that end, we have included a "Joke of the Day" with each Q&A. Yes indeed, a belly laugh a day keeps the marital therapist away!

Here is the layout of the three book series:

Volume One – *Ending The Power Struggle*
Ch 1: "Bruce and Francine's Story" tells our personal journeys.
Ch 2: "Forty-Two Questions from Real Couples and our Answers".
Ch 3: "The Foundation and Pillars of a Strong Relationship".
Here we give the basic principles upon which we answer all the questions. We recommend couples use a process called the "Formal Dialogue" which we elaborate in Appendix 1.
Appendix 1: The Formal Dialogue
Appendix 2: The Theory of Imago Relationship Therapy

Volume Two – *Rebuilding Our Dream*
Ch 1: "The History of Couplehood from the Beginning of Time to the Present" by Harville and Helen.
Ch 2: "Forty-two more Questions from Real Couples and our Answers"
Ch 3: "Creating A Relationship Vision And How To Use It"
Appendix 1: The Formal Dialogue.
Appendix 2: The Theory of Imago Relationship Therapy,

Volume Three – *A New Focus On Each Other*
Ch 1: "Dialogue as Relational Meditation", explains why and how we see the "Formal Dialogue" as a form of mindful meditation.
Ch 2: "Forty-Two more Questions from Real Couples and our Answers"
Ch 3: "Working with requests designed to get your needs met"
Appendix 1: The Formal Dialogue.
Appendix 2: The Theory of Imago Relationship Therapy,

We are hoping that this Trilogy will enhance your intimate relationship and assist you on your journey of growth and healing.

Here's to a thriving relationship, . . . YOURS!

Dialogue as Relational Meditation

This chapter was first published as an article in the
"Psychotherapy Networker" Sept/Oct, 2011

In 2009, we found ourselves at "The Wise Heart and the Mindful Brain" conference, which featured neuroscience expert Dan Siegel, M.D. from UCLA and noted Buddhist teacher and psychologist Jack Kornfield, Ph.D. from the University of California, Berkeley. As long-time couples' therapists, we were attending because we were interested in the insights that neurobiology was bringing to the practice of psychotherapy. We weren't sure about the "meditation" part. We knew that various forms of meditation had become wildly popular as adjuncts to psychotherapy over the past decade or so, but we'd never practiced meditation ourselves. Like many on-the-go practitioners, we'd concluded that we just didn't have time for a meditative practice. Besides, we weren't sure that meditation was relevant to our own work with couples. So we were prepared to wait out the meditation part of the program in order to gather the golden nuggets of neurobiological insights.

Most of the first day had focused on the well-known benefits of meditation: it helps people become calmer, less reactive and defensive, more open, receptive, and compassionate to themselves and others. But the real revelations for us came when Siegel launched into his explanation of the evolutionary and neurobiological implications of mindfulness practice. We learned, for example, that the mechanism by which one of the most common of all mindfulness exercises - focusing on the breath - calms and soothes people.

As Siegel explained it, the human brain evolved as an "anticipation machine," constantly scanning the environment for threats in order to increase the probability of survival – essential to feeling safe. Early humans were able to relax only when the environment looked and felt extremely safe. The challenge for many of us in our twenty-first-century lifestyle is that we have forgotten - or never learned - how to turn off this danger-scanning process. Mindfulness practice can provide a way of doing just that. When you focus on the breath coming in, you can safely anticipate that the next breath will go out, which will be followed by "in" and then "out." Breathing is predictable, so life at that moment becomes safe.

During meditation, when random thoughts enter your awareness, you name them (e.g., "What am I doing for dinner tonight?" or "I wonder why my boss doesn't like me.") and let them go, without judgment. Then you return your focused attention to the predictable pattern of breath after breath after breath. You follow this procedure over and over again. Turning away from the "outside" world and focusing "in close" on breathing, calms the limbic system – the brain's alarm system – thus creating a sense of sanctuary from the storm.

We also learned that focusing on a sensory motor action - like breathing - predicts what Siegel calls the "immediate-next-of-now" and activates the middle prefrontal cortex which is the executive part of the brain. This area, he said, is critical to the kind of emotional states and behaviors that all therapists strive to evoke with their clients: attuned communication, emotional balance, fear modulation, response flexibility, insight, empathy, body regulation, moral judgment, and intuition. Siegel referred to these integrative states of mind as "The Magic Nine."

One brain mechanism that appears central to experiencing the Magic Nine is the firing of the much-celebrated mirror neurons, which can make us "intuit" what other people are about to do or say. When we become calmly attuned to another person, that person will likely become calmly attuned to us.

OUR EUREKA MOMENT!

Halfway through the second day of the conference, Francine leaned over to Bruce and whispered, "Oh my God, what we've been doing with couples over the past twenty years is a form of mindful meditation!" Almost simultaneously, a similar lightbulb went off in Bruce's head as well. On that day, hearing mindfulness practice discussed in a way we'd never heard before, we began to see a connection between what mindful meditation practice is trying to achieve and what we hope to accomplish with the couples we see in our practice. During times of high tension - like your average marital fight - as emotions escalate, partners typically react in anger and fear, doing damage to each other, themselves, and the relationship. But the key to helping partners prevent escalation is to teach them a slow and measured form of dialogue. It takes a lot of coaching and practice, but we've observed over the years that couples who follow the Formal Dialogue protocol consistently (see Appendix 1) feel safer and less reactive together, even during moments of conflict and mutual antagonism.

The more we thought about it, the more it seemed to us that this dialogical practice conferred on couples all the same benefits as meditation - Siegel's Magic Nine, in fact. The big difference, of course, is that two people are engaging with each other in doing this protocol. When most people meditate, they're essentially meditating alone, even if they do it with other people in an ashram or a group and benefit from the communal energy. What seems distinctive about the Formal Dialogue is that it brings mindful meditation directly into what we call "reciprocal relational practice". Each partner is, in effect, focusing on the other's words in a nonjudgmental manner, rather than on the breath or on a mantra. This relational meditative process can develop such a sense of safety for both partners that they can allow themselves to be more fully vulnerable in each other's presence, thus increasing their connection with one another.

At this conference, we recognized that without realizing it, we had been teaching couples to replicate the "immediate-next-of-now" experience. Instead of focusing on the in-and-out of their own breath, however, they concentrate on each other's words during the Formal Dialogue, engaging in a structured process of mutually mirroring each other. They create safety by engaging in the four predictable behaviors of Mirroring, Validation, Empathy, and Response.

THE FORMAL DIALOGUE AS RELATIONAL MEDITATION

The goal of the Formal Dialogue process is to shift a couple from an angry, mutually reactive stance to a calm, accepting, listening one. Being the receiver, learning to Mirror word for word what the other is saying in a neutral and accepting manner without judgment, and learning to Validate, Empathize, and Respond non-defensively, activates the prefrontal cortex just as mindful meditation does. Learning to stay grounded and focused on your partner's words – even when every fiber of your being wants to shout, "Stop! I don't want to hear that! That's not true. I didn't mean it that way. You're taking it all wrong!" – constitutes a powerful meditative practice.

AN EXAMPLE OF A FORMAL DIALOGUE

Here's a Formal Dialogue we had a while back as we were walking hand in hand along the River Seine in Paris. Francine said, "I'd like to have a Formal Dialogue. Is this a good time for you?" Making an appointment is very important to formalize the process and is consciousness raising.

"This is a good time for me," Bruce said. This set Francine up as the sender and allowed Bruce to take a moment to center himself and move into a listening mode as the receiver. Having the sender begin by setting up an appointment for the Dialogue is important so that both parties can prepare themselves to stay in the formal structure.

Francine began with describing her concern about a specific event, "I'd like to talk about your taking 'a day off' from me last week."

Bruce Mirrored what she said, "You'd like to talk about my taking a day off from you last week." Bruce repeated what Francine said word for word, only reversing the pronouns so that she could remain calm in the knowledge of what the "immediate-next-of-now" will be. This format is what keeps the sender feeling safe. It is often tempting for the receiver to change what he or she has heard, subtly reinterpreting what the sender has said or using "better" words. But this only makes the immediate-next-of-now unpredictable and unsafe.

"I really felt awful. I felt punished," Francine continued. Bruce squeezed her hand to signal a pause so he could Mirror (one can also use hand signals for this when sitting and facing each other). "You really felt awful. You felt punished," Bruce repeated.

From there on, we continued the Dialogue in which Francine made her points, punctuated by Bruce's hand squeezes to slow the process down enough to enable him to genuinely hear and Mirror word for word everything she said. The gist of her upset was that by going off by himself for a day, he'd made her feel that he was always choosing the agenda and on that particular day, he was punishing her for not wanting to do exactly what he wanted to do while in Paris.

Born and raised in France, Francine added at this point, "You aren't the king of France, you know. We got rid of kings long ago." A little later, she started crying and added, "I felt chastised, like a child."

The feeling brought back memories of her unhappy childhood with a highly punitive, blaming mother. "Several times, Mom said she was going to kill me and kill herself, and we'd both go to Hell, and it'd be my fault!" Francine explained. Then she said she felt it was hard for her to trust Bruce - she didn't know what he'd done all that day. He squeezed her hand after each remark and Mirrored back exactly what she had said.

Later, after Francine had been silent for a moment, Bruce asked, "Is there anything more you'd like to say about this?" When she answered, "No, not for now," he proceeded to the next step: Validation, in which he as the receiver summarized what she as the sender had told him, and he asked whether his summary was a good summary. When Francine said it was, he continued, "I listened carefully to what you said. Your perspective is important and valuable to me, and you make sense."

During the next step, Empathy, Bruce said, "I imagine you might have felt angry, abandoned, and betrayed by me. Is that what you were feeling?"

Francine said, "Yes, I was feeling angry, abandoned, and betrayed. Right now, I'm feeling heard and calmer." Bruce Mirrored these words once again. He concluded by saying, "Those feelings make sense to me. I can see how you felt/feel that way."

Then it was time for the Response stage, in which the roles become reversed and Bruce becomes the sender and Francine becomes the receiver. Since it's important that each stage of the Dialogue be clearly structured, Bruce began by saying, "I'd like to Respond now," and Francine answered, "OK."

Bruce, the new sender, said, "I'm really glad you asked for a Dialogue. I've been feeling you've been more distant recently."

After a hand squeeze, Francine Mirrored by repeating what Bruce said with the pronouns reversed. "You're really glad I asked for a Dialogue. You've felt that I've been more distant recently."

Two good ways to start a Response are to own what you can own and/or say something like "One thing that touched me in what you said is..." So during this phase of the Dialogue, Bruce told Francine— with each statement punctuated by her hand squeeze to allow what he was saying to come out in manageable, repeatable segments—that he was touched by her tears and passion and that he could really see how hurt she was and how much she wanted to feel connected. He then explained—with Francine Mirroring, word for word—that he'd spent his day alone working on our joint article for the Networker, "messing a bit" with the stock market, and seeing the new Woody Allen movie, *Midnight in Paris*. He added that he had loved the movie and wished so much she could have been there with him. "It included places and museums we'd just visited the day before," he said, and after squeezing his hand, Francine repeated, "It included places and museums we'd just visited the day before." Then she squeezed his hand again and said, "Pause a minute, I need to calm myself."

After her pause to center herself, Bruce said that the day off was helpful to him, that he'd been together with Francine day and night for the previous three weeks on a workshop training tour of Europe, and that he was beginning to feel an uncomfortable sense of being joined at the hip with her. "I think I was too abrupt, and I regret that," he said. "But having more space felt really good!" he added, and Francine Mirrored.

Francine then Validated what he had said by first summarizing it, asking him whether she'd given a good summary – and when he said yes, telling him, "I listened carefully. Your perspective is impor-tant and valuable to me, and you make sense." Following this, Francine Empathized by saying "I imagine that you felt and feel relieved. Is that what you felt/feel?" Bruce concurred, and said, "Yes I was feeling re-lieved and still am." When asked if he had any more feelings to express, he said he felt grateful and connected—which Francine Mirrored, "You also feel grateful and connected. Your feelings make sense to me. I can see how you feel that way."

A STRUCTURED DIALOGUE CREATES A SAFE SPACE TO TALK ABOUT THE RELATIONSHIP

This Formal Dialogue can sound stilted and artificial at first. How can anything good come out of repeating back what each partner says? But paradoxically, the slowness and repetition is part of the strength of the process. Once the Dialogue begins, it flows along, predictably, from moment to moment. The structure of the Dialogue basically ensures that there'll be no nasty surprises, no sudden attacks, and no comments out of left field. Structure equals safety (see Appendix 1 to learn more about the Formal Dialogue – especially the step-by-step chart).

In addition, the tone of voice used in the Formal Dialogue counts enormously. Ideally, it is calm and neutral, conveying nonjudgmental listening without impatient or snarky undertones. The Dialogue essentially holds the couple's interaction in a state of controlled mindfulness, which not only prevents blowups, but also keeps each partner purposefully focused on the other and on what he or she has to communicate. Since the process is predictable and the Mirroring is exact (word for word), each partner knows what's coming next. The limbic system - the primitive part of the brain - is calmed, and the executive functions - the prefrontal cortex - is activated and strengthened. The couple feels less defensive, more relaxed, more attuned and more empathic toward each other. Each partner is therefore better able to hear what the other has to say.

Clearly, we need more research to learn what the impact of the Formal Dialogue is on the brain; however, we know through experience that learning and practicing relational meditation via the Formal Dialogue can have a transformative impact on individuals and couples. Just as it usually takes years of consistent, regular meditation practice to bring about deep, lasting neurobiological changes, practicing the Formal Dialogue won't transform a relationship overnight. We encourage couples to enter dialogical practice with the long haul in mind, just as they would if they were serious students of yoga, meditation, or going to the gym. The life-transforming skills that will heal and change couples take months and years of practice to bear fruit.

As for us – Bruce and Francine – even with many years of using the Formal Dialogue under our belts, we haven't become a pair of saints. We still have disagreements and experience times when we aren't attuned to one another. We've discovered that even when we feel at our best with each other—safe, connected, and close—we can still move into painful disconnection quite suddenly.

It has become clear through scientific studies, that Eastern meditative practices are particularly helpful in calming the nervous system and enhancing a sense of relaxed wellbeing. As we've discovered, alternative forms of structured mindfulness such as the Formal Dialogue can be helpful for couples hoping to explore the heart of their relationship. For further reading, we recommend a book by Buddhist master Gregory Kramer, *Insight Dialogue: The Interpersonal Path to Freedom* (Shambhala, 2007).

2

Forty-Two More Questions from Real Couples and Our Answers

This chapter consists of our answers to questions gathered during two and half years of our "Friday's Q&A Forum for Couples". These are real questions asked by real couples. All the answers are saturated with the principles presented in Chapter 3 of Volume One called, *The Foundation and Pillars of a Strong Relationship*. The goal is to learn how to relate to each other as conscious, committed, intimate and equal partners. Each entry consists of one question sent in by a member of a couple followed by our answer. Our answer is to the person who sent in the question. The answer is not to the couple. This underscores our belief that all couples work is personal work!

Many answers include a brief theory piece, and each has a "Joke of the Day" at the end to help inject some healing laughter into couples' difficult situations. We are confident that you will be able to relate to most of the questions and their answers. Taken together, these Q&A pieces form a practical guide for living together as conscious couples. You may want to read these Q&A's a bit at a time – like a daily reading, allowing you to process the essence of our answers.

Q&A NUMBER 1

Q: I feel discouraged. My husband does not do what he agrees to. I ask and ask, and he says yes – but doesn't do it. Any suggestions?

A: Thank you for raising this issue, which is a perennial problem with many of the couples we work with. Change is difficult and therefore painfully slow. We are all quite entrenched in doing and thinking things the way we do, so much so that we often hear, "Well, that's just the way I am." At one level, this is true, but at another level, this is the way we have become and the way we adapted to our situation as children, and yes, we can change!

We can change if we are willing to learn how. And the most powerful motivator for many of us is our partner. We want to be a good partner, and we are willing to make herculean efforts in order to love our partner the way our partner needs to be loved. But of course, that also is a process. It happens slowly, over time. It requires effort, a commitment to becoming conscious, and a willingness to challenge ourselves to grow. Becoming conscious in our relationship is like learning a new language. It takes a lot of repetition and review until it becomes an integrated part of who we are now.

And we don't want to nag our partner into joining us in this learning process. That would create too much negativity. We've all been there and done that – unsuccessfully. If you are frustrated at your husband for "slipping" or not doing what he said when you made requests before, then hopefully you have written those requests down. Requests need to be written down and dated or it makes it very difficult to review them. Make a commitment to review them in a conscious manner (more on this in the next chapter). We cannot emphasize enough the importance of regular reviews, ideally no less than every other week. Are you doing that regularly?

Cut your partner some slack and give him enough time to change. Do not seek perfection. Look at the direction and give repeated appreciations for movement in the direction you're hoping for. We need encouragement as fuel for the journey.

Lastly, engage in self-reflection as to whether there may be something you are doing that undermines him doing your requests. Receiving love is often difficult for many of us, and drives us to sabotage our partner's efforts.

NOW FOR A BIT OF THEORY

We propose that you commit to the following consciousness-raising practice. In fact, we suggest that you commit to doing them for the next ninety days. Neuroscience has shown that when a new practice is done for ninety days, a new neural pathway is developed in the brain to allow that behavior to become a new habit. Our common culture has validated this by asking AA members to attend ninety meetings in ninety days and by having employers hire new workers for a 90-day trial period. Ninety days is the magic number for consolidating a new behavior.

To help us all grow in our level of consciousness and stay on this journey, we have developed an acronym - THRIVE:

T - Thank & Touch
H - Have a Dialogue
R - Review Behavior Requests
I - Intentionality
V - Vision
E - Eliminate criticism and blame

In the next several Q&A's, we will explain and comment on the components of this consciousness-raising practice.

JOKE OF THE DAY

Some light bulb jokes:

Q: How many Zen masters does it take to change a light bulb?
A: Two. One to change it and one not to change it.

Q: How many feminists does it take to change a light bulb?
A: Ten. One to change it and nine to form a Survivors of Darkness support group.

Q: How many TV reporters does it take to change a light bulb?
A: See the 11 O'clock News.

Q: How many liberals does it take to change a light bulb?
A: None. They don't want to offend the light bulb by criticizing it for not working.

Q: How does Francine change a light bulb?
A: She asks Bruce to change it, and he puts it on his to-do list.

Q&A NUMBER 2

Q: My mother-in-law is driving me crazy! I didn't marry HER when I married my husband. Help!

A: You sound like you are at the end of your rope, and we can assure you that there are many sister souls out there! Conflicts between partners and their family of origin – and sometimes friends as well – are common and thorny. We are faced with holding a delicate balance between current partners, family of origin and how we can integrate both.

The first thing we want to say is that we strongly believe in respecting our families of origin. Our parents gave us life and gave us as much as they could with the strengths and weaknesses and knowledge they had at the time. They have loved us as well as they could, and they have hurt us at the same time. The balance of it all is that we owe them the life we are living now and we want to show them the respect they deserve.

But, what does that mean, "showing them the respect they deserve"? Some of our parents used guilt to control us, and that guilt sticks to us in very powerful ways. They may have used guilt because they felt the intense urge to control us and demanded perfection, because that's the only way they could feel good about themselves. And they try to continue that pattern even after their child, now grown up, marries and lives independently. Some parents feel that just being parents gives them the right to tell their children, adults as they may be, what to do and how to do it. If we feel criticized and unacceptable to our in-laws, it creates painful tension and leads to conflicts in the current relationship.

The two of you need to Dialogue together and design some boundaries that are acceptable to both of you. Come up with a compromise that shows a willingness to stretch and meet the other's needs. Some ideas to propose during Dialogues might be as follows:

- "I would like to limit our visits to your folks to one time a month."
- "When we visit your folks, I would like us to stay at a local motel."
- "I'm going to tell your mother that I like to be in the kitchen by myself. I hope that's OK with you."

The big, big caveat – that which is non-negotiable – is that you never make your partner the bad guy. If you decide to stay at a motel, his parents should never know how that decision came about. Just tell them that you both would prefer it that way and that it's a decision you made together and want to stick to. This means you each own the decision, as being fully your decision, regardless of the amount of stretching it requires for one of you. So don't get seduced into giving Mom and Dad any explanation. Just tell them lovingly and respectfully what you would like to see happen during that visit.

A tall order to be sure! It's a new plateau in your growth journey together, a new step toward cutting the emotional umbilical cord.

NOW FOR A BIT OF THEORY

We proposed in Q&A #1 that you commit to the following consciousness-raising practices, using the acronym THRIVE to help you remember the components of this new practice:

T - Thank & Touch
H - Have a Dialogue
R - Review Behavior Requests
I - Intentionality
V - Vision
E - Eliminate criticism and blame

As mentioned, we will now begin to examine in detail each component of this practice.

T - Thank & Touch

Thank your partner for at least one recent behavior each day. First, make an appointment to do this. We find that making an appointment is a VERY consciousness-raising thing to do. This gets the attention of the receiver, and if they say yes, then they will mirror your thank you in order to let it in. It may sound like the following:

> "I would like to give you a formal appreciation. Is now a good time for you?"
> "Yes, this is a good time."
> "I would like to thank you for taking me to the movies last night."
> "You're thanking me for taking you to the movies last night. You're welcome!"

This goes very quickly AND is a hugely beneficial consciousness-raising practice!

Touch your partner lovingly each day. Hold her hand. Give him a kiss on the neck. Give a hug. Not only is this a consciousness-raising practice, it is also very bonding!

We wish you well on your journey toward bonding through thanking and touching one another.

JOKE OF THE DAY

An old lady goes into the confessional of her church in a small, quaint village.

She says, "Father, I have sinned. I committed adultery."

The priest can tell from the timbre of her voice that she's an older lady. Curious as to who it is, he peeks through the curtain, and says, "Oh, Brigitte, that was 45 years ago!"

"Yes, I know," says the old lady. "But I love talking about it!"

Q&A NUMBER 3

Q: Right now, I feel discouraged and angry. I find it hard to be so careful with my husband all the time. He is always so defensive. I can't bring up anything, and I feel like throwing in the towel. I don't even know that I have a question. I just know that I feel discouraged!

A: Thank you. All of us go through such dark times. We feel hopeless that anything can possibly ever work. We question whether all this hard work is even worth it, and giving up feels like the only solution. We think, right or wrong, I have had it! I'm at the end of my rope. Since this question is so broad and so applicable to many people, we decided to answer it in two parts.

Here is Part One.

We're glad you reached out to us, because the first step in dealing with this, is to let it out, talk about it, and relieve the inner pressure. So scream out loud your inner screams and let your tears flow, all out of earshot of your husband.

Because we live in a world of relationships, it is wise for you to reach out to soothe your inner pain while trying very hard not to hurt your husband. That's because despite all of his defensiveness and maybe precisely because of his defensiveness, we know that he is also hurting. Our behaviors always reflect our inner emotional state, and defensiveness is no exception. This is not an excuse for his behavior. If we could reach a mature level of consciousness, we would not be defensive. We are all responsible for handling our pain in a mature, non-defensive manner, and it looks like he is not there yet. He's not a bad person but a wounded person in the process of becoming the wonderful human being he was born to be.

We, of course, have lots of ideas about Dialoguing and the journey toward intentionality, but now does not feel like the right time. For now, we hope you have one or two trusted friends with whom you can share your pain and your distress. We strongly recommend that you focus on your inner turmoil and stay away from negative analysis of your husband. Try to accept that he is not a jerk (even if he behaves like one sometimes) but instead that he is a wounded child.

Next week, we'll make some more concrete suggestions. For now, love yourself tenderly. Trust that you have in you everything you need to come out stronger and rejuvenated, more enlightened, and able to keep going on your journey of growth and healing.

NOW FOR A BIT OF THEORY

We proposed in Q&A #1 that you commit to the following consciousness-raising practices, using the acronym THRIVE to help you remember the components of this new practice:

T - Thank & Touch
H - Have a Dialogue
R - Review Behavior Requests
I - Intentionality
V - Vision
E - Eliminate criticism and blame

We will now examine in detail another component of this practice.

H - Have a Dialogue: Ask for at least one Dialogue each week. A Formal Dialogue is about a recent event that you want to process (see Appendix 1). It may end with making a request of your partner. We recommend that all requests be written in order to facilitate reviewing them. Have a special clipboard to for that purpose. Changing our behaviors is at the heart of developing a transformed, conscious relationship. And reviewing these new behaviors is an integral part of this on-going process.

Expect that your partner will slip on occasion and still yes, your partner is a good person!

JOKE OF THE DAY

President Obama went to a retirement home to see how his health insurance program was coming along. He bent over and asked an old lady, "Do you know who I am?"
She looked up and said, "Listen, honey. Go up to the front desk and they'll tell you!"

Q&A NUMBER 4
The same question as last time.

A: In Part One of our answer to this question, we mentioned that we wanted to wait until later to make some concrete suggestions. Last time didn't feel like the right time, and honoring that, is part of conscious practice. We can't do good work if the timing is wrong. This is why we make an appointment with our partner before we engage in a Formal Dialogue. Sometimes we hear a client say something like "No use to ask, I already know the answer." Nevertheless, we strongly encourage you to ask. It is your responsibility to ask and your responsibility to accept the answer, "No, not for now," if that's the answer you get.

Those of our clients who Dialogue at home, report that it is often very helpful. They also tell us that it's not unusual for the Dialogue to not go so well, and that it never goes as well as in the office, where it is coached.

With this in mind, here are some pointers that we always track when couples Dialogue in our office.

Choose a very specific topic. Revisit an event that left you unsettled (e.g., "What happened last Sunday morning on our way to church."). Talk about a specific event rather than your general discouragement. This is to help you not make a general complaint about your partner and his or her character. Watch out for analyses of your partner, like "You are so insensitive," "You never . . ." or "You always . . ." Instead, say, "On the way to church last Sunday, you told me I looked like a slob and I felt very hurt and angry. I realize I was feeling rushed and did not spend a lot of time grooming, but your calling me a slob hit me hard." Being the sender in a Formal Dialogue comes with personal responsibilities, namely, sharing your experience related to a specific event and staying away from judgment of your partner. If you blame your partner or attack his or her character ("You're so insensitive!"), that will put your partner on the defensive because your partner will feel under attack.

When the initial receiver becomes the sender during the Response phase of the Formal Dialogue, he or she also has some responsibilities: namely, rather than defending, explaining, or in any way diminishing the experience of the initial sender, the new sender needs to validate it by owning what he or she did say or do that brought about the initial sender's bad feelings. For example, the new sender could say, "I did say that, and now that you bring it to my attention, I can see that you felt hurt. I was being disrespectful, and I regret it." Before the new sender can move into an explanation, he or she must lovingly face what actually took place and acknowledge that with words like "Whether I agree with you or not, whether I intended it that way or not, you, my partner, felt hurt, dismissed, or disrespected by my actions or words." If you can do that for each other, you will make immense progress in your relationship and your partner may become more open to Dialoguing or entering into some dialogical process.

Many times during the Response phase, we, as coaches, don't let the new sender verbalize his or her point of view lest it become invalidating of the initial send. The risk is that the new sender will say something like "Yeah, I did that, but it's because you..." Engaging in that kind of explanation is going on the warpath, which would make the Dialogue unlikely to bring growth and healing into the relationship. It is possible to fight within the Dialogue format, and that is the opposite of what we are trying to accomplish. We are therefore hoping you will be willing to practice SHORT Dialogues at home (no more than ten minutes a send), keeping the above recommendations in mind. Practice ahead of time in your head so you can choose words carefully that will not be offensive to your partner.

We wish you success on your journey toward mature Dialoguing!

NOW FOR A BIT OF THEORY

We proposed in Q&A #1 that you commit to the following conscious-ness-raising practices, using the acronym THRIVE to help you remember the components of this new practice:

T - Thank & Touch
H - Have a Dialogue
R - Review Behavior Requests
I - Intentionality
V - Vision
E - Eliminate criticism and blame

We will now examine in detail the next component of this practice.

R - Review Behavior Requests:

Schedule a Behavior Request Review every two weeks. This is essential to shifting the patterns of the relationship. It is easy to have goodwill and say that you will do such and such for your partner, but following through with this commitment is totally another story. No behavior will change because of goodwill alone. Only staying on top of the BCR Review process will allow new behaviors to actually take root in the relationship, and we believe that no relationship will change unless behaviors change. We recommend putting the BCR Review on the calendar, such as every other Thursday night after the kids are in bed. Or go out to breakfast every other Saturday morning for the Behavior Request Review (see Chapter 3 for a full description of this process).

We wish you well on your journey toward new behaviors.

JOKE OF THE DAY

I needed some time off work, so I decided to act crazy. I hung upside down from the ceiling, and when the boss asked me what I was doing, I said, "I'm a light bulb."

"You're going crazy," he said. "Take a few days off."

I left, and my office mate followed me. The boss asked where she was going.

She said, "I can't work in the dark."

Q&A NUMBER 5

Q: What does one do when one feels triggered? This just happened to me, and I knew I needed to ask for a Dialogue, but it seemed like such a little thing that asking for a Dialogue was making it a bigger deal than I wanted it to be. And yet I could not deny my hurt feelings but did not know how to express them, nor could I hide them when asked directly by my partner if something was wrong. So is there something I can (or should) do myself to get a handle on my feelings in the moments after being triggered?

A: Feelings of being triggered are real, and the temptation to be reactive in the moment is very strong! So the first thing that comes to our mind is to acknowledge to yourself that you do have these strong emotions. It is important that your inner state be acknowledged (albeit privately) without judgment.

And that brings us to our second point. You wrote, "I knew I needed to ask for a Dialogue, but it seemed like such a little thing that asking for a Dialogue was making it a bigger deal than I wanted it to be." You see, what you're doing there is minimizing the importance of what just happened. The importance is not in the factual event itself, actual facts are mostly irrelevant. The importance lies in the impact the event had on you. You felt hurt and triggered, and that's the definition of important. If it hurts one member of a couple, then it hurts the relationship. We like the metaphor, "If you break your little toe, your whole body hurts." If you feel reactive, it is because an event or some words rubbed a raw nerve, and that is important because you are important, not because of your position in life or the income you generate, but because you are a living, breathing person. Take your hurt seriously.

We like your concern that you don't want to make it "bigger than it is," but that is precisely what will happen if you do not deal with the issue constructively (i.e., have a Formal Dialogue). You will be sweeping it under the rug, and that strategy is precisely what will keep the hurt alive. Mistakenly, people often think that talking about an issue will make it worse. But talking about an issue is what makes it better. In fact, it is the only thing that will make it better.

Now, our recommendation does remain that when you talk about it, you choose the right process at the right time, remaining mindful of not blaming your partner but sharing your inner experience instead. If appropriate, end with a request that is positively stated (not "Stop this," or "Stop that.") and that addresses a very specific behavior. We like our couples to say, "I would like you to..." Those words are empowering, and equally empowering is your willingness to accept "No, not for now," should that be the answer.

You will have to develop what works for you during your containment period: a warm bath, going to the gym, practicing yoga, doing meditation, etc. Keep trying until you find the containment technique that works for you.

What we find helpful is to set a weekly Dialoguing time. That will help you contain because then you know you have a time carved out to process any negative emotions. Having that set up will help you relax.

Thank you for a thought-provoking question. We wish you success on your journey to mature containment.

NOW FOR A BIT OF THEORY

We proposed in Q&A #1 that you commit to the following consciousness-raising practices, using the acronym THRIVE to help you remember the components of this new practice:

T - Thank & Touch
H - Have a Dialogue
R - Review Behavior Requests
I - Intentionality
V - Vision
E - Eliminate criticism and blame

We will now examine in detail the intentionality component of this practice.

I - Intentionality:

Give an intentionality that touches your partner's heart each day. We are on a journey from reactivity to intentionality. An intentionality occurs when you gift your partner with a behavior that will touch your partner's heart and entails some form of a stretch, meaning, not something you would do naturally. It is growth producing. We recommend that you tell your partner of your intentionality right after giving them your thank-you for the day. It might sound like "I was intentional for the good of our relationship when I did all the dishes after our party last Friday." Your partner will mirror that by saying, "You were intentional for the good of our relationship when you did all the dishes after our party last Friday. Thank you!" See the introduction of Chapter 3 of Volume 2 for a good explanation of "Thank you's and Intentionalities".

This is a quick, yet profound way to impact your relationship positively.

❦

JOKE OF THE DAY

On Getting Old:
An old lady called downstairs and said, "Honey, come up here and make love to me!"
Her husband said, "Sweetie, decide which one you want. I only have energy for one or the other."

❦

Q&A NUMBER 6

Q: Last time, you talked about containment. Could you please explain what you mean by containment?

A. Thank you for posing a follow-up question. It means a lot to us. It means that you read our Q&A and think about it. We appreciate so much your letting us know that we were not quite clear on that concept. It is particularly important because we think containment is foundational to conscious work. It is one of our pillars of a thriving relationship and it is a difficult skill to master.

This calls for a bit of theory:

Living creatures are designed to survive, and the survival mechanism is automatic. It requires only a split second to react. The human brain is similarly designed. In order to survive, we react. Our reactivity takes us either toward a minimizing pole (pulling our energy back, meaning withdrawing) or a maximizing pole (expanding our energy outward, meaning pursuing). That reactivity gets in the way of intimate relationships in that it leads to disconnection. Since we are human beings and have frontal lobes in our brains that help us think and behave rationally, we have the possibility of countering our reactivity. We call that being conscious, or intentional. That's where containment enters the picture.

Containment means that I consciously, voluntarily choose to do the opposite of what I would do spontaneously. Thus, containment for a minimizing person is to resist the urge to pull away and instead to stay present and engaged. Containment for the maximizing person is to resist the urge to expand energy and instead to remain calm and present.

Ideally, our goal, as we grow and mature, is to contain so well that our partner won't know when we feel angry, hurt, or disrespected. Now containment does not mean that we sweep an issue under the rug. That strategy does not work. Emotions will build up inside and eventually explode in the worst of ways. Emotions need to be expressed and validated so that we don't "lose it" and hurt our partner.

We recommend our couples do their Dialoguing based on the clock, not on what just happened. For example, they could decide to Dialogue every Thursday at 9:00 p.m. for half an hour. In this way, couples contain until their Dialogue time and then they make sure the issue they are containing about is on their agenda. We strongly recommend to our couples that they "sleep on it". We all do much better work when our primitive brain is not activated. Time, especially in the form of time-outs taken with a commitment to contain and process later, is helpful in slowing down and calming our primitive brain.

We hope this helps, and happy containment to all!

NOW FOR A BIT OF THEORY

We proposed in Q&A #1 that you commit to the following consciousness-raising practices, using the acronym THRIVE to help you remember the components of this new practice:

T - Thank & Touch
H - Have a Dialogue
R - Review Behavior Requests
I - Intentionality
V - Vision
E - Eliminate criticism and blame

Let's now look at "Vision" in greater detail.

V - Vision:

We hope that the two of you have created a "Relationship Vision" (see Vol 2 Chapter 3). Read your relationship vision to each other regularly.

Reading your vision to each other is a wonderful way to keep in mind the journey you are on together, and repeatedly reading it out loud helps your brain pull you in that direction. We recommend reading it just before you do other conscious work, such as your biweekly Behavior Review. Also, we recommend that right after reading the vision, you look it over and give an appreciation and an intentionality from the vision. That might sound like "In regard to #4, 'We have satisfying friendships,' I want to thank you for inviting the neighbors over to dinner last night." Then your partner Mirrors that and says, "You're welcome!" An intentionality would sound like, "In regard to #8, 'We lovingly touch each other daily,' I was intentional for the good of the relationship by kissing you on the back of the neck this morning in the kitchen." Your partner Mirrors and says, "Thank you!"

We believe that adding reading the vision, thank you's and intentionalities will add depth and connection to your relationship.

JOKE OF THE DAY

Paddy was driving down the street in a sweat because he had an important meeting and couldn't find a parking place. Looking up to heaven, he said, "Lord, take pity on me. If you find me a parking place, I will go to Mass every Sunday for the rest of me life and give up me Irish whiskey."

Miraculously, a parking place appeared!

Paddy looked up again and said, "Never mind, I found one."

Q&A NUMBER 7

Q: I have heard you say, "Always assume your partner is doing their best!" When I see how my partner behaves, that's a hard assumption to make. I do not think my partner is doing his best. Could you comment on that?

A: Yes, we can. We believe that this idea is SO central to all our growth. If we do not believe that our partner, or anyone for that matter, is doing their best, then we slip into judgment, and if we do, we are on a slippery slope toward judging how others handle their pain. But "best" is relative, fluid, and dynamic, and hopefully, year after year our best gets better.

In our parenting workshops, we use the metaphor of plants, trees and flowers. All of nature strives to be the best it can be, given the nurturing conditions. All plants seek the sun, and they grow and blossom to the degree that the present environment allows it. As living creatures, the same can be said of us.

Francine adds this:

My sweet mother just passed away last Monday, and reflecting on my journey with her, I've been remembering how life-changing an experience it was for me when I finally decided to let it in that hurtful as she was when I was growing up, she was doing her best. Her fears, anxieties, and guilt all got in the way and did not allow her to do better than what she was doing. Only after that truth sank in was I able to develop compassion for her. Only then was I able to let go of my anger and let her off the hook (see Q&A #4 Volume One).

We often say that marriage is a spiritual path. That's because it is amazingly difficult, but growth enhancing, to see that a partner's hurtful behaviors are an expression of pain going on inside (as opposed to being bad).

It sounds like your partner engages in behaviors that are painful for you. Showing soft and loving compassion does not mean that you are okay with your partner's painful behavior. You MUST Dialogue about it, share your pain without criticizing him, or making negative analysis of his character, and make positive requests for different behaviors to replace the painful ones. Use the pain you are experiencing in the conflict to propel you forward to a higher plane.

Be especially curious with what you may have said or done that contributed to the problem. Do this with loving compassion toward yourself, staying away from guilt at all costs. For it is indelibly true as well that YOU are doing your best, even if your best isn't always that great . . . yet.

We are all on a journey toward behaving consciously that will allow our best to unfold and slowly become a healing force in our relationships.

NOW FOR A BIT OF THEORY

We proposed in Q&A #1 that you commit to the following consciousness-raising practices, using the acronym THRIVE to help you remember the components of this new practice:

T - Thank & Touch
H - Have a Dialogue
R - Review Behavior Requests
I - Intentionality
V - Vision
E - Eliminate criticism and blame

We will now examine the last component of this practice.

E - Eliminate criticism and blame:

Put yourself on a path of eliminating all criticism and blame. The way to do this is to replace criticism and blame with curiosity. So instead of saying, "I hate that nasty tone in your voice," say, "I could hear the upset in your voice. I'd love to know what was going on. It sounds like something really got to you." Practice throughout the day, relating to your partner in that manner. We are convinced it will be transformative.

Also, after processing, using a Formal Dialogue, make direct requests that are positively stated and behavioral in nature. This will facilitate eliminating criticism and is a central tenet of our journey. It is equally essential that the requests be written and reviewed on a regular basis (see Chapter 3).

Criticizing each other, which is what we tend to do spontaneously, has and will continue to erode our love and all the good will between us.

Our best wishes for a criticism-free life together.

JOKE OF THE DAY

A Czech man went to the eye doctor to have his vision checked.
The eye chart said: CVKAMWXICTZ.
The doctor said, "Can you read that?"
The man said, "Can I read it? I dated her once!"

Q&A NUMBER 8

Q: My husband feels creatively trapped and stifled by having to repeat back our Dialogue and Mirror exactly. He wants to keep things "loose," as for some reason, Mirroring makes him uncomfortable.

My question is, how important is it for the Dialogue to be exactly Mirrored, and why?

It is my job to make my husband feel safe and secure, and so I do not want to pick this as a battle if it's not necessary. Having said that, I do see the value in my words' being Mirrored back exactly as I express them. I feel like I am trapped between a rock and a hard place on this, and because it does keep coming up, I feel as though it is stopping us from being consistent and truly committed to the process. It seems to me we BOTH have to agree on the process.

A: Thank you for this question. It is a question that is alive in the larger Imago Faculty, so you have your finger right on the pulse!

Let us start with what is noncontroversial. We want to learn to be safe for our partner, but you wrote, "It is my job to make my husband feel safe and secure." We would like to suggest a different concept. It is your job to keep him safe in your presence, both in sending and receiving. How he will feel, however, is not in your court. None of us have the power to make another human being feel something, but we can create a context in which the odds are greater that the other will have positive feelings.

In order to keep him safe, it looks like you will need to mirror him more globally with *paraphrase mirroring*. Paraphrase mirroring is more dangerous to do because it is so tempting to put your own twist on it. But if that is what he would like from you, then that is what he would like from you. The principle remains the same in reverse. His task is to keep YOU safe in HIS presence, and it looks like you would like word-for-word Mirroring. That is your request of him. Ask him to Mirror YOU in the way YOU would like. Come to an agreement about this so that you can Dialogue safely together. If you want to be a source of healing for each other, each of you needs to learn to love the other in the way the other needs to be loved, as a gift of love, not a quid pro quo of "If you . . . then I."

You mentioned that the way you would like to be mirrored makes your husband uncomfortable. That makes sense to us. Growth is always uncomfortable. Another mantra we like is, "My partner's needs are a blueprint for my growth." My growth means I need to modify my character structure, meaning character defenses that worked well in childhood but don't work now. This always puts us in a zone of discomfort. Our hope is that learning to love my partner the way my partner needs to be loved is a strong enough motivator for me to step into my personal growth zone. As they say at the gym, "No pain, no gain!" Few people voluntarily wake up in the morning and decide to start stepping into a new behavioral pattern just because they want to become whole. Most often, the drive to become whole needs a gentle (or not so gentle) nudge from partners and children. Our children are particularly not so gentle, but both of us have felt that much of our growth was grounded in learning to love them, and yes, it was painful, but oh, so worthwhile!

So, put your energies into figuring out what is your need in this situation and what you would like from your partner. Then ask directly and positively for a specific behavior (i.e., "Mirror me word for word.") Your task is not to protect the other (and that includes the children) from the pain of growth. Ask gently and lovingly and let your partner say, "No, not for now," if that's where your partner is at right now. You have the responsibility to ask directly for what you need and the equal responsibility to accept the answer.

Our best wishes to you on that journey.

NOW FOR A BIT OF THEORY

Your question was this: "How important is it for the Dialogue to be exactly Mirrored, and why?"

Our answer is this: "Our words are us!!"

Ancient literature often has this wisdom. In the Bible, the Gospel of John says, "In the beginning was the Word, and the Word was with God, and the Word was God." Words are foundational to who we are. We recommend word-for-word Mirroring because it is so respectful of the other. You ARE your words.

So for example, assume that the sender says, "I HATE your being late because I want you to be a man of your word."

If the receiver mirrors, "I hear you saying that you don't like me being late."

The sender might clarify, "No, I said I HATE your being late because I want you to be a man of your word!"

The receiver would then respond with a true Mirror that honors the sender completely: "You said you hate my being late because you want me to be a man of my word."

As we can see from this example, a word-for-word mirror of our send is more respectful of who we really are. It is a validation of us, and it is letting us be us. Word-for-word Mirroring is much harder to do than paraphrasing because we, as receivers, want the other to be more like us! This is called emotional symbiosis. The difficulty of word-for-word mirroring is that it REALLY lets the other be "an other". We believe that Dialogue is the most powerful method of becoming both connected AND differentiated, the two goals of personal wholeness, and word-for-word mirroring gives a powerful push in that direction.

JOKE OF THE DAY

Waiter jokes:
"Waiter! There's a fly in my soup."
  "OK, I'll bring you a fork."
"Waiter! There's a fly in my soup."
  "Can't be, sir. The cook used them all in the raisin bread."
"Waiter! There's a fly in my soup."
  "Don't worry. It's not hot enough to burn him."
"Waiter! What's the meaning of this fly in my soup?"
  "I don't know, sir. I'm a waiter, not a fortune-teller."
"Waiter! There's a dead fly in my wine."
  "Well, sir, you did ask for something with a little body to it."
"Waiter! This coffee tastes like mud."
  "Yes, sir. It's fresh ground."

Q&A NUMBER 9

Q: Can you go over guidelines for how to respond in a Formal Dialogue? When I share my feelings and my partner responds with "facts" or analysis, I feel betrayed. The safe place of Dialogue suddenly turns dangerous.

A: Wonderful question which many, many couples ask! Just this last Thursday, a similar question was raised in couples' group. We will therefore devote two Q&A sessions to answering it. Here is Part One of our answer.

Part One

Let's go over the guidelines for the Formal Dialogue. There are responsibilities on both sides. The person making the appointment, the initial sender, chooses the topic and is responsible for sending in a manner that does not criticize, shame, or blame the receiver. Because of that, we recommend that the sender revisit a specific recent event, including (if at all possible) specific words or actions involved (e.g., "Last night, you came home from work and went straight to your computer without greeting me. I felt hurt, overlooked, and angry."). Keep the send to that specific event. If you get too broad (e.g., "You are so insensitive and don't care about my feelings," or "You are dominant and arrogant."), your partner will feel that your words are attacks. This will invite a defensive response. We recommend that the send be "an unzipping of the self," a place of vulnerability rather than a character analysis of the other. Character analysis, even with the best intentions, is a recipe for disaster.

Now comes the Response phase, in which the receiving partner becomes the new sender. This also is full of landmines and comes with its own set of responsibilities. When we coach the Formal Dialogue, we insist that the new sender first own his or her contribution to whatever rings true in what the initial sender said. We have found that, the new sender's willingness to own his or her contribution is one of the essential steps toward calming the original sender's feelings (and thus bringing some healing). Now sometimes, much to our clients' dismay, we do not let the new sender do more in the Response phase than own their contribution to the situation, say that they regret what they did or said, and say what they wish they had done differently instead. At other times, it feels appropriate for the new sender to say, "Not as an excuse, but I would like to share with you what was happening for me." For the new sender, it is never helpful to counter the initial send with any kind of logic. Emotions and raw nerves have no connection with logic. None whatsoever! We think that it is disrespectful and fans the fire to say something like, "I can't believe you feel that way," "I didn't mean it that way," "You took it all wrong," or "That's not what happened." All of those statements may be true, but it is unwise to share them with your partner, because if you do, you'll convey a judgment and a putdown of your partner's experience. That is the opposite of what we are trying to accomplish, namely, a kind and loving Validation. (Note: Validation does not mean that you agree!!) So instead, say something like "Thank you for letting me know that you felt hurt. I had not realized that. I love you and I don't want to hurt you. I will work on changing that in myself." This kind of response brings healing in the relationship. Healing is what couples work is all about, becoming each other's healers as we each grow into our higher selves.

NOW FOR A BIT OF THEORY

When we say, "growing into our higher selves," we mean moving from reactivity to intentionality, or moving from unconscious to conscious relating. We need to transcend our feelings and put love into practice. Conscious behaviors have to be put into action before we necessarily "feel" like it. Feelings follow behaviors, not the other way around.

We wish you the depth of healing that your committed relationship can bring you.

JOKE OF THE DAY

Did you hear about the Buddhist who refused Novocain during a root canal? He wanted to transcend dental medication.

Q&A NUMBER 10
Q: Same as the last question.

A: As mentioned in the previous Q&A, the question of guidelines for the Formal Dialogue responses comes up so much that we decided to devote two Q&A forums to it.

Here is Part Two of our response.

Just last night, a couple at a session was asking "But when do I get to give my perspective?" We think we can all identify with that. We are filled with emotions. We feel like we're bursting at the seams, and we want to relieve that inner tension. To take care of this inner sense of urgency, we recommend shorter sends. For a loaded topic, we think a ten-minute send should be the max. But sometimes in the office, we go sentence by sentence until the couple is back in balance. That doesn't change the rules for responding to the sender in a conscious and in-tentional manner, but before the Responder (the original receiver who is now the sender) gives his or her perspective, we must make sure the original sender feels really heard and validated.

We lead Responders into first owning what they can, telling them to say, for example, "I own that I slammed the door and said I was done," or "I own that I did say, 'You are just like your mother.'" Then we coach them into saying something like "I can see now how hurtful and threatening that was to you. It makes sense to me you felt hurt and accused," or "It makes sense to me all your abandonment issues were triggered. I regret having said those words. In the midst of my anger, I said things I now genuinely wish I hadn't said. I wish I had contained better. I wish I had asked for a time-out instead."

Sometimes, the Responder cannot say any of the above words. Their perspective is SO different that validating the perspective of the original sender feels simply impossible. So we coach the Responder to begin a Response with something like "Something you said that touched my heart is that you really want to work through this issue together and that you want to learn to become a safe partner for me." We think it is a good practice to find something positive to start with, to be affirming of our partner, and to share gratefulness for the process as well. The Responder can do this last part by saying "Thank you for raising this issue in Dialogue form. It feels safer to me." Sometimes, that's all we let our Responders say. It's a clinical judgment call. Sometimes it feels right to leave it there. Other times, we lead them to say, "I would like to tell you what was happening for me." This is also a judgment call. You don't want to come across as defensive. When you explain yourself, you may often sound defensive. You might well have to explain yourself in another Dialogue another day. But you might instead say something like, "While I am not proud of my reaction, when you showed up forty-five minutes late to our date, my emotions boiled over and I felt unimportant and abandoned." Possibly this could be deepened if it is all about you and not blaming the other.

We think it is important for the Responder to not come from a defensive place, to explain what happened to them while still holding themselves accountable, giving an explanation, not an excuse.

We believe that it is essential for both partners to gradually move from, "My reality is the only worthwhile reality," to "I am curious about what it's like to be you, and I want to move to a place of honoring and respecting what it's like to be you."

We hope this helps, and we wish you well on your journey of learning containment and giving and receiving Validation and Empathy.

NOW FOR A BIT OF THEORY

We more and more are coming to see that not only are there two sides to an issue, but both partners contribute 50/50 to every conflict. We often like to think it is 80/20 or 60/40, but we feel it is much safer to assume it is 50/50 and then to try to reflect on what your 50 percent contribution was rather than who is at fault.

~ ❧ ~

JOKE OF THE DAY

A college professor called on a pharmacist. "Give me some prepared tablets of acetylsalicylic acid," he said.

"You mean aspirin?" asked the pharmacist.

"That's it. I can never remember that name!"

~ ❧ ~

Q&A NUMBER 11

Q: My wife has decided to file for divorce. After we attended the couples workshop, she chose not to make any effort in Dialoguing positively or sharing frustrations in a Dialogue. Instead, she chooses to put forth her efforts in badmouthing me to anyone who will listen. She spends her time watching every negative show on television, and she calls me disrespectful names. Now that she has decided to file for divorce, I've become more joyous and begun working out. She chooses to put forth no effort but chooses trivial matters as her focus. She is very, very violent, and we share a child. What should I do?

A: It sounds like a painful end to a painful story. Not what you had hoped for! So you're asking "What should I do?" We certainly don't want to be preachy or trite, but we are willing to make a few suggestions.

The first is to accept what is. In your case, your wife has chosen to file for divorce. You have to grieve and mourn the loss of what could have been and never will be with her. These last two words, *with her*, are very important because our failure in one circumstance of our life does not mean a failure in everything else. You can say, "I, myself, am not a failure, but it is true that I, myself, have failed at this one life endeavor." So do not put yourself down. Instead, treat yourself with gentle kindness, saying "At this point, it looks like I have failed at my marriage with that person. I need to face that in a loving and compassionate spirit toward myself, also courageously facing what I can learn from the divorce." We like to tell clients, "There are no mistakes if we are willing to transform them into stepping stones toward learning, becoming bigger, and stretching toward our better selves."

In your case, the fact that you have a child together may motivate you to transcend whatever vengeful thoughts you may have. You tell us that she badmouths you to everyone willing to listen. Ouch! That hurts and probably feels one sided and unfair. Your challenge, at this point, is to not retaliate. Share your pain with a trusted friend. Share your pain in a vulnerable way, without crossing the line of badmouthing her. This is particularly salient because you have a child together. Both of you are this child's parents . . . forever! Make a commitment to yourself to never speak negatively about your child's mother to the child. The child loves you both, and you want to make sure you don't put him or her in a position of having to take sides. That is way too anxiety producing for a child.

Lastly, we are making the assumption that you did not go for regular coaching after the weekend. Wonderful as the weekend is (and we do believe it is wonderful and a potentially life transforming experience, thanks to Harville and Helen!), for most of us, it requires ongoing practice. It is the practice of Dialoguing that will transform your relationship. We still have issues that come up (even after twenty-five years of couples work), and we Dialogue about them faithfully.

If your partner does not want to Dialogue, then we recommend that YOU become "dialogical." That means that you become a good listener and you validate and empathize with your partner. (Note: Validation does not mean that you agree!) If one partner makes a shift, the dynamic of the relationship changes. Just one person can change the course of the relationship.

It may be too late for this relationship, but we hope that you will be able to make good use of the life lessons this divorce is offering you, particularly by lovingly facing the answer to the questions, "What are my contributions to this divorce? In what way did I feed the pain in our marriage?" If you can gently and courageously look at that, then you have the possibility of not repeating the past in your future.

We wish you strength as you find direction in your life!

NOW FOR A BIT OF THEORY

You might not want to hear our piece of theory today.

We strongly hold the view that BOTH partners in an intimate, committed relationship contribute equally to conflicts. When conflict seems one sided, it is suggested that you pause and take a long look at yourself and work on owning YOUR contribution. This often makes all the difference in softening the other side.

❧ ❧

JOKE OF THE DAY

What did the Leaning Tower of Pisa say to Big Ben?
"If you've got the time, I've got the inclination."

❧ ❧

Q&A NUMBER 12

Q: What are some of the key characteristics that define an Imago Match vs. a relationship that isn't an Imago Match? Or would the Imago theory claim that all committed romantic relationships are Imago Matches? If memory serves, I believe I heard Harville once say, "We meet, fall in love with, and marry the person least capable of meeting our needs." Again, if I remember correctly, that's not a statement that would apply across all romantic relationships. Or would it?"

A: Wow, you are someone who does a lot of theoretical thinking! While understanding theory does not heal, we human beings are curious and seek to understand and make sense of our lives.

The characteristics of an Imago Match are that we are intrigued with someone, are increasingly attracted to that person, keep dating each other, and eventually decide to be a Committed Couple. In our current culture, that could mean marriage or moving in together and planning a future together. So yes, Imago theory states that if you move in together, you are an Imago Match.

We agree with Harville's statement that if we are in a committed relationship, we are with a person least able to meet our needs. This may provoke incredulity at first. How can this be? It is so because during the romantic period, while courting one another, we are so focused on meeting each other's needs that initially, our relationship feels like a match made in Heaven. And it is! It gives us a taste of what it's like to be loved, to feel treasured and appreciated, and to have our needs met.

During that romantic period, we think our partner likes what we like, thinks the way we think, and wants to do what we want. It is a period during which we are all forgiving and more than ready to interpret our partner's behavior in a positive light. We more or less spontaneously assume the best of each other. The key word here is *spontaneously*. We "project" (a technical term) all sorts of positive qualities onto our partner. But then things gradually (or not so gradually) change as our commitment deepens and we discover that this wonderful partner of ours, with whom we have fallen in love and voluntarily moved in with or married, is a different person from us! And then we start saying things like:

"I can't believe . . ."
"You've got to be kidding . . ."
"You always . . ."
"You never . . ."

In other words, we criticize the other for not being us! In fact, unconsciously, we fell in love with that person because he or she was not us! We fell in love/moved in/married precisely because that person was primarily wounded at the same stage of development as we were and adapted in the opposite manner. One person carries the minimizing energy, the other the maximizing energy, so together we are whole. The best image we can think of is the Yin-Yang symbol. Our defensive adaptations are not noticed during the romantic stage (or they don't bother us). Now, as commitment deepens, comes the work of growth and healing—that is, accepting the other as "other," which we believe is achieved by practicing the Imago Processes we teach in the workshop, our private sessions and our groups.

We believe the above comments apply to all romantic relationships. This is the chemistry of romantic attraction. Now, this does not necessarily apply to one-night stands where, attracted or not, we want to play around. It is possible that some people were less wounded during childhood and will find another person who is also not very wounded. If such people become a couple, they will not experience the tension and the power struggle to the same degree as a couple that is more wounded.

It would be nice if a very wounded person would be attracted to and pair up with a less wounded person, but unfortunately, it does not work out that way. We are coupled up with a person who is primarily wounded to the same degree we are. Otherwise, we lose interest in each other. The good news is that with regular practice of Dialogical work, we can become a source of healing for each other.

We wish you well on your journey of understanding, growth, and healing.

NOW FOR A BIT OF THEORY

The Imago (a word for *image* in Latin) is an internalized, composite image of all the positive and negative traits in our parents and primary caretakers. It is like a metal detector similar to those used on the beach to find coins and hopefully lost diamond rings. The earphone buzzes every time metal is detected. When we leave our home of origin, the Imago is a detector that buzzes every time we come across an Imago Match. One would think that we are looking for the positive traits of our parents. But it is exactly the opposite! We are looking for the negative traits. Of course, this is VERY unconscious – and this IS the chemistry of romantic love.

The reason for this is that we have a deep yearning to grow, heal, mature, and become whole. Therefore, we unconsciously team up with a person who will trigger all our unfinished business so that we can grow and heal. It is always painful to be triggered by our partner, but remember Imago's mantra: "Conflict is growth trying to happen." If our partner had all the positive traits of our parents, we would not be in a position to grow up and finish childhood.

JOKE OF THE DAY

A man saw an advertisement in a paper that read, "Porsche for Sale: $200." He went round to view it, expecting to find a battered heap of rust – but instead, he found himself looking at a gleaming new model in mint condition.

"Why are you selling it for $200?" he asked the woman who placed the ad.

"Simple," she said. "Last week, my husband ran off with his secretary. He said, 'You can keep the house, but sell my Porsche and send the money on to me.'"

Q&A NUMBER 13

Q: In your consciousness-raising acronym, THRIVE, the letter E stands for "Eliminate criticism and blame." But how can I eliminate criticism and blame if my partner is hypersensitive to criticism and blame? In fact, to her, "everything" is experienced as criticism and blame. I find it extremely difficult to address negative things because regardless of how I try to say it, it's almost always received as criticism. Frequently, it's easier to say nothing at all.

For example, we had some cash that we discussed leaving in the house as a small emergency stash. When my partner told me she'd spent it, I said, "I thought we agreed to leave it in the house in cash?" That's all it took for her to get defensive and accuse me of criticizing her. It happens frequently, and this is a pretty minor example.

A: Thank you for a very thoughtful question, and for spending time reflecting about the acronym THRIVE (from Q&A Number 7) and various Imago principles.

As a general guideline, we like the phrase, "Eliminate all criticisms." On the practical level, it is a journey, a process that we will probably be working on till we die. First of all, if you were raised with criticism (and most of us were), you have probably developed hypersensitivity to criticism – which means that you will be drawn to the interpretation, "You are criticizing me." It sounds like that's true for your wife.

The second point is that criticisms can be very subtle. Some criticisms are direct and very much in your face: "You are such a _____." (Fill in the blank.) But other criticisms are embedded into more vague sentences that look "innocent," like the question "Did you fill the gas tank like I asked?" Our psyches are very attuned to and ready to negatively interpret a statement that even remotely smells of criticism.

We think that your statement, "I thought we agreed to leave it in the house as emergency cash," belongs to the second category. It is a vaguely veiled criticism. Clearly, you were not pleased with what you discovered. That makes total sense to us. You have the right to feel upset or at least displeased. What matter is how you handle your feelings.

Learning to handle negative emotions in an intentional manner is a cornerstone of Imago work. We think that intentionality begins with containment. Containment is not sweeping your emotions under the rug, like you seem to sometimes do since you said, "Frequently, it's easier to say nothing at all." This has been shown over and over to be a failed technique. To hold off (contain) until the right time, using the right process, is much more productive! We strongly recommend that you avoid raising a potentially contentious issue in the moment and contain till the time is right.

In your case, part of handling the situation in a conscious manner would have included your realizing that that topic was probably emotionally loaded. That would have prompted you to keep your own reactivity at bay. Then a day or so later, you would have asked for a Formal Dialogue. Many of us do much better, in terms of listening and validating, when we are in the safe structure of the Dialogue.

When you "say nothing," that is unconsciousness calling you. It is easier for you to say nothing, but it is worse for the long-term health of the relationship. The road to consciousness is always more uncomfortable and even painful, because it requires that we enter an "unnatural" zone. This unnatural zone includes a total acceptance of the "otherness of the other". While I myself wouldn't react that way, my partner did. Part of it is "her stuff", and the other part is mine. What did I do? What could I do differently next time? Maybe in a Dialogue, you could say, "I like having some emergency cash around the house. Would you be willing to talk about it before you spend it? I am willing to do that and it would mean a lot to me, and I would feel safer if that were acceptable to you."

It may not be that simple, in which case you need to do even more Dialoguing about it. Keep validating each other and over time, a solution will emerge. Remember to write requests down and review them regularly to keep the requests in your consciousness (see Chapter Three).

What happened to spontaneity, you ask? It simply does not work!! Spontaneity is wonderful for the fun stuff, but NOT for the painful stuff!!

Keep Dialoguing!

❧⚬⚬❧

JOKE OF THE DAY

The company accountant is shy and retiring. He's shy a quarter of a million dollars. That's why he is retiring.

❧⚬⚬❧

Q&A NUMBER 14

Q: Hello! I am curious about the concept that we are all equally wounded in childhood. It makes sense that we are all wounded, and I know I have childhood wounds, but with all the troubles going on in the world, I can't imagine that my wounds are as bad as those of other children. Could you explain?

A: Yes, we can explain! Thank you for giving us the opportunity to clarify what we mean.

We believe that to some degree (from a little bit to excruciatingly so), we have all suffered some as children. We have all suffered some because our parents were and are human. They have their own hurts and pains and unfinished business from their own childhood. They also had a life to live – sleeping, showering, going shopping for the family, cooking, and possibly going to work. So they could not be available for us just at the moment we needed them. In other words, at the very moment we needed Mom or Dad or someone, life was happening. This prevented a nurturing adult from being reliably available to us, and consequently, pain entered our lives.

Because pain entered our lives, we all developed protective mechanisms, protections that allowed us to survive and reach adulthood, albeit more or less emotionally broken. Some of us minimize our energy in the presence of danger, others of us mobilize our energy and become "energetically big." One adaptation is not better or worse than the other. Both hurt the partner and hence hurt the relationship. So we enter adulthood with some woundedness, and we have adapted in a manner that kept us alive in childhood. But now, as adults, this adaptation gets in the way of our intimate relationship.

The concept of equal woundedness comes in when we understand that we are attracted to a person who is wounded to roughly the same degree as us and who has adapted by developing the opposite energy from us. (We call that "Matched Woundedness/

Complementary Adaptations.") One of us is a minimizer, and the other is a maximizer. We are not all equally wounded as children in the world. The concept of equal woundedness is only for those who have fallen in love with each other and have stayed in the relationship until full commitment is made. When we fall in love, we experience wholeness because together, we are whole. Then gradually, the adaption of the other becomes unacceptable to us and we begin to criticize the other for being different from us. We call that being emotionally symbiotic and, in our unconsciousness we launch on a journey of trying the get the other to see the world OUR way and become more like us.

These concepts are very useful as you begin a journey out of reactivity and into intentionality together. This is the process of breaking the symbiosis. Most of us find it so easy to think the problem is the other and that "You hurt me more than I hurt you." Instead, stay grounded in the foundational knowledge that we contribute to problems 50/50 and that "I am 100 percent responsible for my 50 percent". That means that I have to be willing to dig into myself and own how I have contributed to any point of tension between us.

Overall, then, the concept of equal woundedness applies to couples, not to everybody in the world.

Hope this helps!

❦

JOKE OF THE DAY

John decided to use the word *penis* for his password to get into his computer. The computer responded with "Too short. Choose another password."

❦

Q&A NUMBER 15

Q: I recall you both talking about the importance of a one-way send, saying that if both partners are triggered by something, there should be two separate Dialogues. When we Dialogue with one-way sends, I feel heard and cared for and I feel able to extend compassion and a willingness to stretch to meet my partner's needs.

Is it possible we are not yet ready for two-way sends? Or is it a part of my growth to be present to hear my partner's needs even when I am hurt and triggered? Maybe it is a healthy boundary for me to not want to hear my partner's needs in an Imago Dialogue in which I am a very hurt sender?"

A: Well, this is a big, big question our clients raise very often. There is no one-size-fits-all answer. So much of it is a judgment call, a tailor-made response to each particular Dialogue. Still, there are some general principles to guide us in our decision process.

First, by definition, "having a dialogue" implies that two people are involved and that they both have the opportunity to speak. If a partner feels that she or he will be unable to hear an answer (which is perfectly OK), then we recommend you ask for a a Mini-Container (more about that in NOW FOR A BIT OF THEORY).

Also, let's get well grounded in knowing what the goal of the Imago Dialogue is. It is to break the emotional symbiosis, meaning to break the feeling in most of us that "I need you to see the world my way." This breaking of the symbiosis requires both differentiation and connection. When I send and my partner Mirrors and Validates my perspective, it feels wonderful. That's the connection part. Telling me that I make sense puts salve on my emotional wound. In an ideal world, this empathic validation allows me, the initial sender, to be emotionally present for my partner, who now becomes the new sender. Of course, we do that more or less well. All of us are challenged to be a good receiver for the sender.

A good receiver is one who is EMOTIONALLY present and remains neutral. That process of listening to our partner's different perspective is precisely what builds our inner strength and grows us into a differentiated Self. Differentiation does not feel as good as connection, but it is what breaks the symbiosis. Initially, this is hard work – and for some of us, it is very, very hard work. But not listening to our partner's perspective as he or she responds will only slow the whole process of becoming conscious.

Francine remembers that during some Dialogues, listening to Bruce's perspective was excruciatingly painful. She remembers thinking "The hard work of getting a PhD is nothing compared to listening to Bruce's perspective when I disagree with it." But she had asked for a Dialogue, and by golly, she was going to follow through and make it to the end.

Now, there are rules – yes, rules – for a successful Dialogue. In sending, we strictly require that there be no shaming, blaming, or negative analysis of the other. We tell our clients to focus on the mantra, "I assume the best of my partner. My partner is a good person, albeit hurt and handling the situation poorly (unconsciously)."

Then we ask the Responder to start with owning what he or she can, saying things like "I did yell at you. I did call you names. I can see that saying _____ was a putdown, and it makes sense to me that you felt _____." This step is very, very difficult, and the Responder may not do it perfectly. But the Responder should always try. It is important for partners to be encouraging and receive each other where they're at. And if the Responder adds anything to the Dialogue, it is very important that it not be a justification or a defense. This would only invalidate the initial send. The Formal Dialogue is a process, a journey, and partners need to receive each other with grace.

What we absolutely would not want the Responder to say is something like, "I did this because you . . ." or "Well, you're not perfect yourself!" Giving an explanation or a justification just tends to invalidate the initial send and the entire first half of the Dialogue. What we would accept and encourage is vulnerable sharing—something like "I feel badly that I raised my voice and left the room. I do wish I'd had the strength to stay and remain engaged. I was so flooded with fear, and I felt so threatened. I feel very vulnerable in this area." The Responder deserves to share his or her emotional turmoil or state of panic and pain, and he or she also deserves a hearing and empathic validation.

One beautiful aspect of the methodology we use in working with couples is that when one partner grows, the other heals. In the Formal Dialogue, the roles of sender and receiver change so that both partners experience the benefits of growth and healing!

Hope this helps!

NOW FOR A BIT OF THEORY

It is especially important that when you ask for a Formal Dialogue, you speak about a specific event.

If you want to feel heard and do not want to hear a response other than empathic validation, ask for a "Mini-Container." This may be new to some of you because we do not present it in the workshop. A Mini-Container consists of a short send, no more than two minutes. The receiver Mirrors, Validates and Empathizes, then the sender may or may not make a request concerning the issue being addressed. Here is what a Mini-Container sounds like:

Sender: *"I would like to have a Mini-Container. Is now a good time for you?"*
Receiver: *"Yes, this is a good time for me."*
Sender: *"I feel really hurt that you came right home and forgot to stop and get some milk. I called you at work to remind you. It's a crucial ingredient in my recipe for our guests tonight. I hate it when you forget my requests. I feel unimportant to you and insignificant.*

The receiver gives a summary Mirror rather than a word-for-word Mirror, which would break the flow of the sender's emotions. Then the receiver asks if it's a good summary and Mirrors any additions given by the sender. The receiver Validates and Empathizes in the standard Formal Dialogue format. The whole process must not take more than three minutes. It can end with a request, for example:

Sender: *"I would like to ask that you go right now and get some milk. Would that be OK with you?"*

The receiver Mirrors and hopefully grants the request.

The crucial element in this form of Dialogue (the Mini-Container), which we want to emphasize here, is that everything is wrapped up in less than three minutes. This has proven very helpful to us, to take care of immediate tension when we don't have time to go into a lot of depth and still want to handle our relationship in a conscious manner. Remember, no shame, blame or criticism still holds!

This comes with our best wishes as you continue your journey toward developing a conscious relationship.

❧❧

JOKE OF THE DAY

How many men does it take to change a roll of toilet paper? We don't know – it's never happened!

❧❧

Q&A NUMBER 16

Q: During some of our couples' group sessions, you recommended not saying "sorry" to your partner and not asking your partner to apologize. Can you elaborate on why this is not advised and perhaps give an alternative to apologizing or asking for an apology?

A: Very nice question. Most people are surprised when we recommend not saying, "I'm sorry." It certainly deserves an explanation.

Let us first say that under the right circumstances, we do believe that apologies are appropriate. But apologies in our culture have been overused and often used inappropriately. Very often, apologies (especially "I'm sorry") are what we say when we want to get off the hook. Often when we say, "I'm sorry," we're really saying "OK, I said I'm sorry, so now let's move on!" It tends to be a kiss-and-make-up move designed to just get over it because (we believe) it's no big deal.

But often, the person who felt offended does not feel better after that kind of apology. That person is more likely to feel dismissed or maybe even judged for having emotions relating to the issue at hand. It is not unusual that one partner, complaining that the other keeps bringing up old stuff, says, "I don't know how many times I have to apologize." If that happens, it means that there is still unfinished business.

Why would there be unfinished business despite many apologies? Because before we apologize, we must own what we did in a sufficiently detailed manner. So we should not say, "I'm sorry I hurt you." That is a cheap apology because it is so vague and general. An apology is worthwhile only after the apologizer recognizes and states what he or she did that hurt the partner. A proper apology sounds something like this: "I interrupted you and you felt belittled and unimportant. I regret that I did that. I can see now how that felt rude to you. I apologize for that. I wish I had stayed quiet and let you finish your thought." An apology like that, which the apologizer should make after owning his or her behavior, will most likely feel sincere to the one being apologized to and will likely facilitate that person's forgiveness of the offense.

But often, we follow up our apologies with a defensive response or an explanation that immediately wipes away whatever apologies we made. It is also not uncommon for us to say something like, "I didn't mean it that way. You took it all wrong." That is the ultimate insult and denial of our partner's hurt feelings. Our partner may be more than willing to accept that we didn't mean it that way because we probably didn't. However, whether we meant it or not, our partner feels hurt – and for the moment, that's what matters. It is quite common that we hurt one another unintentionally. Words, behaviors, and gestures sometimes have unintended consequences. To become intentional (the goal of relationships), we want to accept that we did hurt our partner, so instead of giving explanations, we should acknowledge our hurtful actions by saying say things like "I DID hurt you and I truly regret it. I love you and I don't want to hurt you." Then and only then can we apologize in a manner that will feel authentic and true.

We have one last concern about apologies. Often, one partner asks for an apology from the other with the implication that the other is the guilty party. They usually say something like, "You owe me an apology!" And we can imagine some situations in which that would be true. For example, if I went out with some old friends from college, drank too much and got into a car accident, then that would be 100 percent my responsibility and I would absolutely owe my partner an apology! But in a relationship, both partners contribute to conflict. They share responsibility for each conflict, so if one partner apologizes, the other should as well – and both should state very specifically what they're apologizing for.

Those are our thoughts on apologies. Hope it helps!

JOKE OF THE DAY

A man's credit card was stolen, but he decided not to report it because the thief was spending less than his wife did.

Q&A NUMBER 17

Q: Our Dialogues at home go quite well during the first part, but later, it all falls apart. Any pointers you may have would be appreciated.

A: This is probably the most frequently asked question. This is where the challenge lies: It is sometimes easy to agree to an Imago Dialogue because we do come from a place of goodwill, but then it is easy to become flooded with emotions during the Dialogue and lose our groundedness.

The initial sender is somewhat at an advantage. She or he chooses the topic (remember, only one topic per Dialogue). The initial receiver, on the other hand, is doing the very difficult work of Mirroring neutrally, which means having to practice a lot of containment, deep breathing, and thinking "I want to be a good listener for my partner." Indeed, many Dialogues do go well right up to the Response, when all hell may break loose. Clients have described such a scenario many times. The first receiver, now the sender, has been under so much pressure doing the containment that once released to Respond, he or she can easily explode. Also, the new sender may mistakenly think that the Response phase is the time to set the record straight. This leads the Responder into the trap of starting to explain and justify his or her behavior, thus invalidating the notion that the partner felt hurt in the first place.

We often feel the urge to clear our name. This is particularly true if we were raised with a lot of guilt. So sadly, some Dialogues we have observed simply have become new forums for fighting. The Responder might say, "I didn't say that," or "I didn't do that." And then moves on to a negative analysis of the other, the Responder might continue with, "You always twist the truth," or hurl back a counter-accusation like "You're never on time yourself!"

So we need guidelines to accomplish a constructive Dialogue. A Dialogue is not a structured forum for a fight but a structure in which to hear one another including something we disagree with. It becomes imperative to watch the words we use. That is what we mean in Imago when we talk about becoming conscious. The ground rule is that the sender must not criticize, shame or blame the receiver, neither in the first half of the Dialogue nor in the Response.

Here is an example of an unconscious send we recently heard in a Dialogue: *"You chattered constantly. Every thought you had came out of your mouth."*

We had the sender resend this in the following way: *"For whatever reason, on our way here, I experienced your talking as constant chatter. I regret judging you for that. I wish I had said, 'Honey, given the mood I am in right now, I would like us to sit here and drive in silence. I hope that's OK with you.'"*

That would have allowed the sender to share his inner experience and ask positively for a different behavior.

We do realize that without a coach, it can be very difficult to do this. Even with a coach, it's hard! So remember to keep the sends brief to very brief. Remember also to share your inner experience instead of analyzing the character of your partner.

Thank you for sharing with us that you are taking the process of Dialoguing seriously and that the process is challenging. We like that we are a community that can fully identify with you and that you can feel free to share with us openly.

NOW FOR A BIT OF THEORY

The couple's journey is from reactivity to intentionality, meaning from unconsciousness to consciousness. This is bound to be a difficult journey. We are hardwired to be reactive in order to keep ourselves safe. We have evolved to reflexively duck in order to dodge a bullet – and in addition, we have married the enemy, meaning we have partnered up with an Imago Match, someone who has the negative traits of our parents, making our spouse the very kind of person who will trigger all our reactivities.

Of course, the reason we unconsciously chose an Imago Match is that it puts us within the possibility of the deepest growth and healing, thus making couplehood much more difficult than remaining single. Imago Therapy is, we believe, the best program to help us learn how to move into conscious living.

∞

JOKE OF THE DAY

A man walked into the lingerie section of a store and asked the saleswoman for a nice bra.

"What size?" she asked.

"Seven and three-quarters."

"How did you measure it?"

"With my hat!"

∞

Q&A NUMBER 18

Q: When we visit my husband's family, I feel a lot of pressure to do things the way they want. I am working on setting boundaries for myself in a healthy way. My husband is happy to go along with many of his parents' expectations, though, so I often look like the problem person who is pulling away from family togetherness. Francine has advised us to form a united front as a couple, so we work together ahead of time on establishing expectations before we go visit the in-laws. But there are many situations that come up during a visit that we didn't anticipate, and since our instinctive responses are the opposites of each other, our united front collapses. How can we handle these surprises?

A: We love this question and are surprised it hasn't come up more often, because situations such as you describe arise frequently. They arise with in-laws and extended family members and between parents and children. The technical term we would use is triangulation. Triangulation creates a two-against-one alliance. Triangulation is absolutely destructive in family relationships and in human relations in general.

On the other hand, congratulations on working ahead of time, as a couple, to decide how to handle these predictable situations. But as you pointed out, life happens, bringing about many unanticipated situations.

So what could you decide ahead of time? The one guiding principle we are recommending is that your husband remain neutral and absolutely (yes, absolutely) not cast aspersions on you. Whatever he says to his parents, his parents shouldn't know his position. That may be a tall order, but we think it is essential if he is going to keep you safe. You need to trust that come what may, he will never cast you in a bad light.

So what might he say? Perhaps "Thank you, Mom and Dad. That's a lovely idea, but I want to think about it first." It is especially important that he not explain his position. He does not need to justify his decision to hold off giving an answer, but he does need to hold on to his decision lovingly and neutrally. It would be especially important to stay away from saying "It's OK with me, but let me check with my wife." Ouch! That would hurt you and feel like a betrayal. Neutrality IS the operative word. Let's say they pushed a bit and asked why. For this situation, practice a sentence along the lines of, "I'm not comfortable with making a decision right now. I want to think about it some more." Memorize this sentence so it can be available in the midst of pressure. Now, let's imagine someone says, "Oh! I get it. You don't want make a decision without her consent!" It could even be a bit sarcastic: "Oh! She runs the show, doesn't she?" Do not rise to the bait. Simply and calmly state, "I want to think about it some more before I give you an answer." Remain neutral. Do not let them know your position—and yes, your thinking can (and should) include your partner if you're going to present a united front, but you don't have to explain how you make your decisions. That's your private business.

To feel good about ourselves, some of us need to feel liked. So we are willing to compromise our integrity in order to give an answer that will please the other. Not pleasing our parents, in your case your in-laws, puts us at risk of being labeled as bad, resistant, weak, or whatever word carries a sting. For some of us, that's unbearable. Given the Imago mantra, "My partner's needs are a blueprint for my growth," if your husband can learn to meet your needs and remain neutral (which may displease his parents and trigger his fear of being a "bad" son), he will experience growth and you will experience healing. That's a win/win!

Of course, what is implied here is that the two of you would Dialogue about how to handle the unexpected situations. Read this Q&A aloud to each other and see if the above ideas might work for both of you. But in general, say no to triangulation and yes to a united front!

We wish you well on your journey of learning to honor each other.

JOKE OF THE DAY

After twelve years of analysis, I finally was able to get in touch with my emotions and break down and cry. What happened? My analyst looked at me and said, "No hablo inglés."

Q&A NUMBER 19

Q: I find questions (and especially a lot of them) to be exhausting. If there are no plans, often one of us will ask the other what he or she would like to do, and that is often followed with a question, and then a question regarding the question (e.g., "What do you think/feel about that?").

I find this tiring, and I recall your saying something about problems with questions. Can you please explain if and when questions are ever appropriate and what you would advise?

A: We love your description of a question about a question followed by more questions. And like apologies, questions are sometimes, loving, caring, and appropriate. But also like apologies, questions can faintly hide attacks or criticisms.

The main problem with questions is that they put us on the defensive. If we are asked too many questions, we feel as if we are sitting in the presence of a prosecuting attorney. It makes us feel like our motives, character, thinking processes, and critical judgment, are all being scrutinized. And for many of us, it triggers our insecurities and gets us off kilter, making all our self-doubts bubble up even if our partner did not intend it. But it is not our partner's intentions that matter. What matters is the effect his or her words have on us. Each of us must know that we are all wounded children, and we must want to develop a compassionate listening style.

Also, asking questions is a powerful way to avoid vulnerability. I, as the person asking questions, am in a superior position. I am the boss, and the boss is allowed to ask questions of subordinates—just as the teacher asks questions of students, and just as parents ask questions of children. Asking questions tends to establish a hierarchy, and that's something that we in our work with couples are trying to break in our attempt to establish equality in committed partnerships.

We recommend a different approach. We have found that most questions can be transformed into statements. So don't ask, "What do you want to do?" Instead, say, "I would like to propose that we . . ." This approach makes the speaker become much more vulnerable by taking a risk that his or her partner might say no. This is also better than asking a question, because a question can be received as a demand. But a statement will not be received that way unless it is a demand! And therein lies a potential pitfall. In a couple, both must agree that a proposal is just that: a proposal, meaning something they put on the table to work from, tweak, and chisel until both feel OK about it, something that may not be exactly what either one wants, but it is a loving compromise both can live with.

Now, after making and responding to such a statement, either or both partners may well have unanswered questions. So it is wise to develop alternatives—softer wordings for statements that may still include questions. For example, one could say things like, "I'm not sure I follow you there. Could you tell me more about what you have in mind? I can sense this is important to you, but I am uncomfortable with some of the plan and would like to propose this instead." Take a risk! The worst that can happen is that your partner will say, "I would rather not," or "No, not for now."

So while we do believe some questions come from a genuinely loving, curious place, questions can carry significant triggers and it seems wise to replace questions with statements. Doing this increases the sender's vulnerability, and learning to be vulnerable with each other will increase closeness and connection.

NOW FOR A BIT OF THEORY

The operative Imago principle here is that we must strive to keep our partner feeling safe at all times. If I am unhappy, I must learn how to communicate that safely. If I am angry, I must learn how to deal with that safely. The bottom line is no criticism, shame, blame, or acting out.

When you want to talk about something your partner has done, describe it the way a video camera would record it. Do not interpret it. For example, rather than saying "You hurt me when you criticized me," say, "I felt hurt when you said I had ill will toward you." Don't ask a question like, "Why did you come home late last night?" Instead, say, "I felt hurt and unimportant when you came home after 7:00 p.m. yesterday."

We wish you well on your learning to choose the right words.

JOKE OF THE DAY

If there were an animal called a Yabba Dabba, and if you decided to keep it as a pet in your backyard, then you would eventually step in Yabba Dabba Doo!

Q&A NUMBER 20

Q: I am very discouraged. Everything is falling apart. Maybe I'm too nice. Is it possible to be selfless to a fault?

A: Well, like everything else, it is possible to do anything to the extreme. And extremism in any form is going to have a negative impact, which is what you are describing as happening in your life.

Let's look at your behavior—"being selfless to a fault"—from a psychological perspective. Those of us who tend to engage in this behavior were raised believing we were bad or deficient in some way. We are then driven by guilt and a strong desire to show and prove that we are good, worthy people. And therein lies the problem: We engage in all our good behaviors from a place of weakness as an attempt to redeem ourselves. So we do good, do good and do good some more. But doing good is often not so much a source of healing for an other, as it is a source of soothing relief for our battered self-esteem. We feel so unworthy that we forget to include our own needs in the balance.

Therefore, our goal on our maturing journey is to become assertive. Assertiveness consists of stating our needs directly and positively in a manner that is respectful of both, ourselves and others. Keeping our needs and others' needs in balance is tricky and precarious, so the child in us prefers an all-or-nothing approach. Classically, we always say yes to the requests of others without considering our own needs. Two things happen then: 1) we become resentful rather than fully owning our decisions, and eventually, others feel our resentment and direct it back at us until we explode at them; and as a result, 2) others lose respect for us. They know we are pushovers and will use that against us, and this is why we feel abused. But just as others may be abusing us, we are abusing ourselves.

The way out of this dilemma is to learn to set boundaries—lovingly, respectfully, and firmly. You need to have clarity with your limitations saying, "I wish I could do that, but I am not available." Many people need coaching to learn how to establish their boundaries, and they need support to develop the kind of inner strength it takes to lovingly say, "No, not for now."

On the other hand, be aware that by setting your boundaries, you put the relationship at risk. Many people don't like facing boundaries, especially if your new boundaries represent for them a shift from the way you used to be. First, you hear the message, "You must change!" But then when you change, you hear the message, "Change back! Before, I could manipulate you, but you are developing inner strength now and I don't like that!" Realistically, at that point you don't have a relationship anyway. You feel overwhelmed and beaten up! The truth is, no relationship will ever work out well unless the partners learn to set their boundaries in a loving and considerate manner. That's because there can be no connection without differentiation, and the Self can emerge as differentiation grows.

Happy differentiation to all of us!

NOW FOR A BIT OF THEORY

Pia Mellody says, "All relationship problems are boundary problems." The root of the issue is this: it is scary to set boundaries because it always puts the relationship at risk—but if you don't have boundaries, you can't have a healthy relationship, and the relationship is still at risk!

Shouting "I AM ME!" does not help you develop a Self. Instead, empathically validating your partner creates a Self for you. Letting your partner be an "other," letting him or her be "not you," brings about differentiation—and along with that, a Self can emerge. I am, and who I am is not you, and that allows you to emerge as a worthwhile person. This will eventually give you the strength to set boundaries for yourself, meaning you will be able to say, "No, not for now." Mirroring your partner accurately with empathic validation, even when you deeply disagree, brings about differentiation. That is the first and essential step on the journey into Selfhood.

❦

JOKE OF THE DAY

Marriage is like a poker game:
It takes a pair to open.
He shows her diamonds.
She calls his bluff.
They end up with a full house!

❦

Q&A NUMBER 21

Q: I often feel criticized and am not sure how to respond. What is the correct response if your partner attacks your character?

A: We like this question and would also like to broaden it, as it covers areas that are ever so present in our work with couples and our supervision of students. We are thinking of situations where one member of a couple in a Formal Dialogue is not containing well (e.g., rolling his or her eyes, making faces). In spirit, the response to these situations is always the same—the ball is still in your court. Let us explain.

Our deep desire is that our partner will change, that our partner will stop attacking our character and will take us, and the Dialogue process seriously. Oh, how we yearn for that! It would make things so much easier. Parents have the same wish. If only their children would do what they were asked to do, in just the right way and at just the right time! In other words, we all want the OTHER to do the changing.

With our mates, our children and our colleagues, we yearn for an easy solution. But there is no easy solution—and that's a good thing! The highest purpose of our lives is to mature, grow, change and evolve into a better self, and that can only happen when we have our back against the wall. So nature provides us with endless opportunities to strengthen our "maturity muscles." From a practical standpoint, this means that we develop enough inner strength to put limits, OUR limits, on a situation. We must say things like, "This is not working for me, so I am going to take a time-out," and then we must DO IT! We must disengage, go take a bath, go to the gym, go practice yoga, etc. But instead, most of us try to control our partner's behavior, saying "Do this—don't do that!" Trying to control another is a lost cause. For one thing, telling your partner not to do something is negative and critical. Your partner will respond with defensiveness and a desire to rebel. It will not foster cooperation.

Your task is to ask positively for a behavior that will begin to take care of your needs. Make requests like "When we are in a Formal Dialogue, I would like you to keep your face and voice neutral when receiving." or, "I would like you to agree to a twenty-minute dialogue once a week on Thursday night, after the children are in bed." or, "I would like you to share about specific behaviors I engaged in that hurt you." Then end each request with "Would you be willing to do that?" Remain courteous and kind, even if your partner is not. Your task is not to be nice if your partner is nice. Your task is to be nice regardless of your partner's behavior—not because of, but in spite of—because that's the only way you will grow!

Needing to take care of yourself and learning to set boundaries for yourself, making requests on your own behalf without trying to change the other, would sound like: "I am finding those words offensive. I feel under attack. This is not working for me, so I'm going to take a time-out. I'd like to revisit this tomorrow, when I feel calmer." Please be prepared for the fact that setting your own boundaries will be very difficult and that your partner may not react well to it—because once you learn to set your limits, you will not be so easily manipulated. On the other hand, there is no other path to maturity. We often tell our clients, "You will be respected to the degree you respect yourself. The journey starts with YOU."

Our best wishes on your road to self-respect.

NOW FOR A BIT OF THEORY

Last week, we quoted Pia Mellody, who said, "All relationship problems are boundary problems." But setting boundaries is not enough! Before you can set boundaries, you must take a deep breath and contain your reactivity. Then you need to take action. If at all possible, give Empathic Validation, saying things like "That comment I made really hurt you.

I regret saying that." If you can't do that, then take a time-out as described above. And be aware that taking a time-out is not withdrawing. Withdrawing is being reactive, while taking a time-out is a positive step forward. Taking a time-out is not sweeping the issue under the rug. It is waiting for the right time to bring the issue up in a formal Dialogue.

JOKE OF THE DAY

Marriage changes everything. Suddenly, you're sleeping with a relative!

Q&A NUMBER 22

Q: When you request a Dialogue and your partner says, "No, this is not a good time," should you try again later? or does the onus fall on your partner to suggest another time that would be better? What is a reasonable time interval between an initial request for a Dialogue and when a Dialogue actually occurs?

A: These are frequently asked questions. On the issue of who is responsible for follow-through when a request for a Dialogue is denied, this is what makes sense to us: The person who initially asked for the Dialogue has the energy and the drive for that Dialogue, so that person should be responsible for the follow-through. It is the initial requester's issue and the initial requester who feels the need. That's whom the motivation lies with. So we recommend that the initial requester not turn their power over to their partner. The partner has no emotional investment in having that Dialogue, may not have any idea what the Dialogue will be about, or may have an idea and therefore may not look forward to having that Dialogue. So the long and the short of it is that whoever's issue it is, that person needs to follow through.

You then ask, "What is a reasonable time interval between the initial request for a Dialogue and when a Dialogue actually occurs?" We feel uncomfortable with the word *reasonable* because reasonableness is subjective. Only the partner receiving the request knows what is reasonable for him or her. So it is our task—difficult and challenging to be sure, but still our task—to accept our partner's subjective reality as what's reasonable. With practice and a desire to get over the hump, we gradually begin to see the reasonableness of our partner's perspective. Sometimes a partner says, "No, not for now," because he or she is on the way out the door. In this case, there is no psychological component to the answer, "No, not for now." At other times, a partner gives this answer primarily for psychological reasons. But in either case, we would definitely suggest sleeping on it and waiting for the next day before having that Dialogue.

We also recommend setting fixed times for your Dialoguing. Reserve half-hour slots on your calendar for Dialoguing at times that work for your family. Knowing that there is a fixed time for a Dialogue coming up on the calendar will help both of you contain until that time. We have found that demanding a Dialogue right away when you become upset will most likely lead to disaster.

Once a couple is in a Dialogue, they must eliminate accusations, shame, blame, and analyzing each other's character and motivation. Many couples try to do this but often fail. We have found this to be the main reason why partners refuse to engage in the Dialogue process. Also, the Dialogue process can be misused—turned into a long, searing session of, in effect . . . "I feel that you are the worst creature that ever walked the face of the earth!" The sending partner also often feels unsafe if the receiving partner makes faces or smiles during a send. When this happens, the sending partner feels belittled, dismissed, and/or disrespected. That is why we coach our couples in word-for-word Mirroring and in remaining neutral, present, and warm. Ultimately, a successful Dialogue is not just about following a set of rules or a script (although that helps guide the process). The success of the Dialogue lies in our willingness to "listen with our hearts" and let our partner's reality penetrate "the crust of our own self-involvement" (to borrow a phrase from Daphne Rose Kingma).

We wish you well on your Dialoguing journey!

NOW FOR A BIT OF THEORY

The Formal Dialogue teaches several very basic things about safe communication:

1. You must take turns: only one person speaks at a time (no interrupting).

2. When sending, put aside all criticism, shaming, or blaming.
3. When listening, contain all reactivity. Stay present, warm, and connected.
   Listen with the heart!
4. When Responding, start by owning your stuff.
5. Learn how to Validate even when you disagree.
6. Learn how to Empathize by guessing the feelings of the other.

These things can ONLY be learned through practice a few times a week. Goodwill and book learning will not give you these skills.

∞♾∞

JOKE OF THE DAY

A man brings his wife a glass of water and two aspirins.
She looks surprised and says, "I don't have a headache!"
He says, "A-ha!"

∞♾∞

Q&A NUMBER 23

Q: My partner has expressed the idea that people are who they are, and I get a sense he thinks most people don't change. So I am wondering about the part of Imago that states one partner must fundamentally change to help the other partner heal his or her childhood wounds and become whole again. I understand that when we are wounded as children, we suppress part of ourselves as a way to protect ourselves. I also understand how accessing that suppressed part of ourselves can be a healing thing. I understand all this in the abstract sense, but I have a hard time seeing this in reality. I guess I am looking for an example that would help clarify the idea for me and help my partner see how Imago views making changes.

A: Thank you both, not only for your question but for thinking through the implications of the Imago theory—the nitty gritty of those Imago concepts that are the underpinnings of the practical work we do.

Your partner's belief that people are who they are is one we encounter frequently, but we believe it to be an illusion. People are what they have become as a result of their early childhood experiences interacting with their own inherited biology. It is usually accepted that some very basic psychological traits are well established by the age of six. After six, change must be remedial, coming in the form of therapy or a dramatic change in parenting style. But six is very, very young, and we are under the control and influence of our primary caregivers—usually our parents. If they did a good job the first six years, chances are they will continue doing a good job. But even if they didn't do a good job, it is most likely that our pattern during our first six years will continue and we will continue to adapt in order to survive. We may not thrive, but we WILL survive!

Our survival, however, is at the cost of our full aliveness. At a very young age, we learn that parts of us are unacceptable, and we use our life energy to hide rather than be fully alive. This is what Imago refers to as *childhood woundedness*. To some degree, we believe that we have all been wounded and have some sense of inadequacy, some fear of being judged as not acceptable. So we block out the daily pain of believing that we are flawed. We convince ourselves that "That's the way it is. This is me—take it or leave it." But in reality, this "me", is a somewhat broken me, but it's been me for so long that it feels like the real me. The good news is that we can go beyond "the me" that we have become as a response to childhood experiences and go toward the me we were born to be, with full access to our life energy. That is one of the goals of therapy.

And the even better news is that in Imago, we believe that being in a committed, intimate relationship is the deepest form of therapy! Love will stretch us to the furthest limits of our being. Love will ask us to be bigger, stronger, more courageous, softer, gentler, and slower—to go where we never dreamt we could go. One of our mantras in Imago is "My partner's needs are the blueprint for my growth." This works because we fall in love with complementary energy: one of us is a maximizer and the other is a minimizer, one of us is very rational and the other is full of emotions, one is very organized and the other might be more bohemian, and one is anxious and the other is laid back.

For example, twenty-five years ago, Francine was very quick to anger. During this time, Bruce used the Dialogue to ask Francine for specific behaviors that would help him feel loved. So day in and day out, Francine chose to work on her anger in order to love Bruce the way he needed to be loved—and eventually, the miracle did happen! This took a lot of work, as Francine's anger was rooted in the fact that her mother was very anxious, guilt ridden, controlling, and punishing. But when Francine chose new behaviors in order to love Bruce the way he needed to be loved, she also became a more whole person, gaining access to the calmer, softer part of herself.

For Bruce's part, his work to love Francine the way she needed to be loved has been to become more present and learn how to be more validating of Francine's perspectives. Francine's call to greater acceptance helped Bruce become less judgmental and more empathic, his own judgmental nature having roots in the fact that he was raised in a very judgmental fundamentalist Christian home as a missionary kid in China.

We have observed these complementary dynamics in all our couples, so the question for all couples is "Am I willing to learn to love my partner the way my partner needs to be loved?" If I am and I start engaging in the behaviors my partner asks me for, then I will change. I will grow beyond myself as I meet my partner's needs, and when my partner does the same for me, I will experience healing."

The "dance" for all Imago couples is this: While one grows, the other heals.

We wish you well on your journey of growth and healing, and in your dance of personal development.

⸎

JOKE OF THE DAY

"I tried to kill myself yesterday by taking 1,000 aspirin."
"What happened?"
"Oh, after the first two, I felt better."

⸎

Q&A NUMBER 24

Q: The other day, my wife and I were catching up on our day and things were wrapping up. Her final remark was "Last chance to notice my new dress." Clearly, I had messed up and I felt ashamed for not noticing. I am aware that when things like this happen, I begin to feel on edge that I will miss something else and I feel mildly paranoid about it. Can you offer any wisdom on how I can deal with this trend in our relationship?

A: How to clean up whatever mess we may have created? Certainly a worthy question—worthy because the only prediction we can make with 100-percent accuracy is "We will slip up!" To think that we won't is simple arrogance. We will slip up, not because we have bad intentions but because we have not arrived at full consciousness yet. We are in a process of becoming conscious. This is a dynamic process that, we hope, will only end when we die.

So you slipped. You didn't notice her new dress. She now has an opportunity to be conscious and relate to you in a mature, adult, intentional way. This would sound something like "I just bought myself this new dress, and I am disappointed you didn't notice it." She may add "I want to be attractive to you, and I love to get compliments from you." Well, remember, she is in the process of becoming conscious also, so instead, she made an underhanded comment, one that hurt you and that is a reflection of her hurt. (Were not taking away the sting of her comment, just giving it its psychological meaning). Out of hurt comes more hurt as long as we remain unconscious and reactive.

So you both slipped up, but now comes your opportunity to be bigger than yourselves and transcend your reactivity. For you, that means learning to Mirror the emotions you heard your wife express. Even though she did not express them directly, they were there beneath her words. Do not start with an apology, especially a trite one such as "I'm sorry." That would likely pour fuel on the fire. Start with ownership and empathy, saying something like "I didn't notice your new dress and you're feeling hurt about that. You're trying so hard to please me, and it probably looked to you like I was oblivious to you and maybe insensitive. I feel bad about it, and I regret that I didn't notice your new dress." Don't overdo it lest it sound insincere, and don't become defensive and give explanations for your behavior. Instead, stay focused on the hurt of your partner since she opened that door. Stay with her and postpone dealing with your feelings until the next day or the day of your scheduled Dialogue. Notice that we say "postpone," not "sweep it under the rug." When you ask for a Dialogue the next day, you might make a request like "When I fail to notice something that's important to you, I would like you to tell me directly." Explain to her that this would help you relax, instead of having to perform a high-wire act. Let her know that you are committed to growth and taking her needs seriously—and let her know that what would facilitate that process for you would be her commitment to telling you directly, lovingly, and in a non-shaming way that you have failed at something. That would allow your energies to shift from protecting yourself to noticing her more.

Now, what we just described is difficult to accomplish. Maybe the best you can do is to remain quiet. Because silence can be heavy with judgment, tell her "I am being flooded with emotions right now, so I am going to remain quiet for a bit." It would be ideal for the two of you to agree on that strategy ahead of time. But don't forget to process the incident consciously so you both grow on your journey of becoming.

NOW FOR A BIT OF THEORY

When in an Formal Dialogue, you Mirror word for word so that your partner can feel fully heard and taken seriously. When not in a Dialogue, like in the situation above, you want to "be dialogical." When you do this, you don't mirror the content of what the other said, but you mirror the emotions behind the other's words. For example, you might say, "You feel disappointed I didn't notice your new dress. I often don't notice things that are important to you. I plan on making progress." Save the explanations for another day—but for sure, process the incident!

JOKE OF THE DAY

Did you hear about the scientist whose wife had twins?
He had one baptized and kept the other as a control.

Q&A NUMBER 25

Q: For most situations at this point, I feel ready and prepared to use the tools that I have been gaining through Imago. Of course, I do slip up and need to get back on track often, but I can always see where a tool should be used without excuses! But I lose hold of the Imago practices when I see my husband lose his temper with our children. I simply cannot wait for him to cool off and be respectful of him and the mood he is in when he is making our child a victim of his rage.

As a mom, I feel compelled to come to the aid of our son and basically pull him away from his father. I want our son to know and trust that at least one of his parents is still in a place of consciousness and that he is not at fault in any way. I would even hope my husband would do the same if I went off the rails, so that we as a team could always be consistent in showing our children the difference between right and wrong.

Of course, my husband interprets my response to his anger as throwing him under the bus. So how can I use the Imago skills set as a guide for how to act when he goes ballistic on the very person we are trying to model to and protect? In that moment, my priority becomes our child and I just don't care about anything else.

A: This is a question that tears at the heart. We feel for you in your horrible dilemma. You are truly caught between a rock and a hard place because there is no good solution, only the least bad one. Life can be horribly complex, and we are often faced with choosing from a palette of undesirable options.

Given your situation, you need guidelines to help you choose a course of action. You said, "My priority becomes our child." We find this to be a good starting point. The question is what action is actually worse for your child: letting his dad rage at him or stepping into the conflict yourself? We believe that in the long run, presenting a divided front to children will have more negative consequences.

Why do we say that? Children are masters at "divide and conquer," and if the parents let them, they will use it liberally. Unfortunately, it gives the children undue power and will leave them feeling insecure. They need to trust that Mom and Dad are the co-captains of the ship and that they're not divided as to where they're going. We believe that an undesirable parenting technique is to spend the day putting out the fires as they arise. It only creates chaos, and while the child may temporarily enjoy his power, he will end up feeling unsafe and guilty.

The problem you are facing is a marriage problem, not a parenting problem. The problem is between you and your husband, so make a commitment not to drag the children into it. Come what may, the two of you need to have many Formal Dialogues, making requests that are positively stated, such as "I would like you to apologize to Timmy for yelling at him Monday night, in front of me." Make sure you practice asking positively. Eliminate negative statements like "Stop doing that," or "Don't do that." That will help you practice being a safer mom and will help you make positive requests of your children.

We recommend that you have weekly "family roundtables," as described in Francine's book, *Raising Cooperative & Self-Confident Children* (Pasadena Press, 1997). Beyond that, make sure you and your husband do lots of Dialoguing. Tell him how it hurts you when he loses his temper with your child. Tell him what your fears are. Listen empathically to him. What's happening inside him when he gets angry? What are the triggers for him? As you observe your husband "losing it," remember that he is a wounded child. Stay there, in the presence of your husband and child, as a silent witness. Keep your heart open to both of them. As Richard Rohr said, "Unless pain is transformed, it will be transferred." That's what you are witnessing with your husband. To pull your child away from his father's behavior at that moment, will negatively impact both your husband and your child. Ultimately, your best strategy is to learn how to be a source of healing for your husband.

Also, when your child comes to you, it is essential that you do not take sides, even subtly. Stay out of it and Mirror the emotions of your child neutrally and warmly, without any hint of negativity toward your husband. The issues between you and your husband need to be taken care of privately and in a dialogical manner.

We believe that your husband needs to experience from you what you would like your child to experience from both of you: warmth and compassion, coupled with clear limits.

That's what we believe is best for your child.

❧

JOKE OF THE DAY

Two dogs were walking down the street when one suddenly crossed the road, sniffed a lamppost for a minute, then crossed back again.

"What was that all about?" asked the other dog.

"Just checking my messages."

❧

Q&A NUMBER 26

Q: I think my husband is seeing someone. He denies it and blames my suspicions on my childhood because my father was a philanderer. In the workshop, you said children of alcoholics often marry alcoholics and children of abuse often marry abuse. Since I'm a child of a philanderer, maybe I married a philanderer. I'm confused on how to handle this. Should I just blindly trust him? How should I handle my suspicions?

A: Affairs (including emotional affairs) do rear their heads regularly, and they arouse anxiety and anger in many marriages. In a unique way, affairs provoke deep feelings of hurt and betrayal in those who believe their relationship is based on monogamy and exclusivity.

We obviously don't know what's happening with your husband, but what we do know is that some things he does make you feel uncomfortable and arouse your suspicions. So first, we would not recommend that you blindly trust him. That would be a betrayal of your own needs and an act of self-disrespect. In the long run, nothing constructive can come out of that. Sweeping stuff under the rug and ignoring what your emotions are telling you can only (in our experience) make things worse between the two of you. Ultimately, we believe that moving toward transparency is the solution to the underlying mistrust you describe.

But (yes, there is a "but") how you go about dealing with this delicate subject is of primary importance. You have to bring up your suspicions with him in order to deal with them, but if you accuse your husband, it will trigger his defensiveness, whether or not he is having an affair. Many of us felt unjustly accused as children and carry a deep wound about that. Also, in addition to his pain from his wound from childhood, you have probably done and said things that trigger him. We are not saying that your frailties give him permission to find solace outside the relationship. They don't. We're not saying he handled the situation from a conscious perspective. He didn't. What we are saying is that when you approach him, you should make a huge effort to be gentle with him. Also, keep in mind that, in some way, and you may not know how yet, you contributed to his distress. So be gentle with yourself as well—gentle and tender yet fearlessly honest with yourself. But make sure to only bring such a delicate topic up in an Formal Dialogue. Describe the behavior that concerned you during a specific event, and then end the Dialogue with making a positive behavioral request. This is more difficult to pull off at home by yourself. You may want coaching for this.

Examples of such requests could be as follows:

- "For this coming week, I would like you to come home by 7:00 p.m. to have dinner with me."
- "When you come home this week, I would like you to turn off your phone."
- "I would like us to sit down together for thirty minutes twice a week for the next two weeks to talk about our day, after the children are in bed." Always end with "Would you be willing to do that?"

Do not skirt the issue of a possible affair, but do not accuse him. Tell him that because he does such and such (e.g., being gone several hours without calling you), you feel suspicious. Ask him if instead he would be willing to do something like calling you to let you know what he is doing and when he will be home. Tell him, "Because I love you, I want our relationship to grow, and I want to deepen my trust in you, this is something you could do that would help me on my journey of learning to trust you more."

We wish for you to have the strength to tackle the issue openly and directly as well as softly and lovingly for both of you.

NOW FOR A BIT OF THEORY

Imago theory postulates that all couples want two things: safety and passion.

Passion is not a hard sell. You are all probably saying, "Yeah, I want that!"

Research in the animal kingdom shows that, passion emerges only in the presence of safety. Therefore we make the notion of "Keeping my partner safe in my presence" a central element of the work we do with couples.

Keep your partner safe by clarifying in Dialogue form events that left you feeling uneasy and learn how to do it without criticizing or analyzing your partner.

Enjoy the passion that will be the by-product of safety in your relationship.

❦

JOKE OF THE DAY

A duck walked into a store and bought some lipstick.

"That'll be $3.99," said the cashier.

The duck said, "Put it on my bill."

❦

Q&A NUMBER 27

Q: My wife gets very defensive when I share my feelings with her. She always interprets me as criticizing her. For example, when I ask when she will be ready, I'm just innocently making plans—but she feels that I'm upset at her for being late. I feel stuck. I just want to have normal conversations without her getting so defensive all the time.

A: Thank you for such a pertinent question. It is perhaps the situation we encounter the most. By far, most of us come from a good place in the heart. We want to be helpful. We want to solve the problem. We share the knowledge we have, but then our partner is less than thrilled about receiving all our wonderful input. And why does he or she react so defensively to our innocent questions?

The problem lies on both sides of the equation. If your wife feels criticized, chances are she felt criticized as a child and was wounded thereby. She is therefore primed to hear your comments or questions as criticism. But on the other side of the equation, your words probably have a critical overtone. You may have convinced yourself that your questions are innocent, and maybe they are. But she won't perceive them that way unless you choose your words very carefully to sound noncritical.

So, to avoid this problem, we recommend that you don't ask questions. Generally, questions make us feel unsafe and put upon. They make us think or say, "I am experiencing you as so invasive! You want to know too much! You'll use it against me somehow, sometime, someday, so I better protect myself and keep my mouth shut." We raise this issue in our parenting workshop. Well-meaning parents ask their children questions in an attempt to connect and show they care, but instead of answering the questions, the children clam up, especially if they are teenagers.

The other thing that brings a negative reaction is the well-meaning offer of advice. Our goal in Imago is to love our partner the way our partner wants to be loved. That's the challenge! But often, we give unasked-for advice that results in the recipient thinking things like *My partner must think I am stupid. I figured out that answer on my own! I just wanted a sympathetic ear, a listening heart that was willing to patiently hang in there with me.* We all need to believe that our partner has the answer. If they don't, they will ask us unless they are afraid that we would shame them in some way.

Lastly, let us emphasize that sharing negative feelings is a sure way to give rise to defensiveness and disconnection. Sharing negative feelings is absolutely an implied criticism!

So, what should you do? Listen without giving your opinion unless specifically asked, replace questions with a warm Mirror of the emotion being expressed, and replace sharing feelings with making positively stated behavioral requests. For example, "I'd like to leave by 3:30, would that work for you?" We think practicing these techniques will greatly decrease your partner's defensiveness and actually begin to heal that wound of hers. That's the beauty of Imago work with your partner. As you learn to decrease questioning and learn to Mirror emotions (instead of judging them), you'll experience growth and she'll experience healing. And growth and healing are the journey toward consciousness.

Now, how could you do a better job of asking when she will be ready? The two of you need to sit down ahead of time and decide when you need to leave in order to get to your destination on time. You need to decide together what works for both of you. Once you've done that, you must trust that she will be ready on time. If she isn't, ask for a Dialogue about that at your next scheduled Dialogue time. Don't raise your concerns in anticipation. She would experience that as you not trusting her word. Take the risk she might be late, and Dialogue about that one instance if that were to happen.

JOKES OF THE DAY

1. What's the difference between a cat and a comma?
   One has the paws before the claws and the other has the clause before the pause.
2. What happened when the cat swallowed a penny?
   There was some money in the kitty.

Q&A NUMBER 28

Q: My wife had an affair, and after several years of Imago work, I have come to understand part of how my own insecurities contributed to this terrible chapter of our relationship. Before the affair, I had been largely content with our sex life. In the course of therapy, she explained that the sex in the affair was fantastic and that clearly she was not the problem with our sex life. While I know my insecurities preceded our relationship, I feel caught between knowing that my insecurities partially caused the affair and feeling like the affair confirmed my biggest fears about myself. How can I overcome my insecurities without ignoring that I failed to be an adequate sexual partner for over a decade without even being aware of it?

HELP!"

A: It sounds like you and your wife are emerging from a very dark tunnel. You have been shaken to the core and still need to process what happened. Here are some of our thoughts: Your wife fell in love with another man and the sex was "fantastic." When we are in the romantic "in love" stage of a relationship, sex IS fantastic. Our blood is saturated with feel-good hormones and it is heaven on earth! Researchers have compared it with a cocaine high. But then, as with all drugs, the effect tapers off, and we go back to baseline. Your insecurities undoubtedly played a role in the affair, but so did hers. A profound concept in Imago work that has been transformative for both of us is that we contribute equally to the problems in a relationship. In a committed, intimate relationship, we have insecurities and fears that may be quite different but that weigh us down equally. We also hurt one another equally. At a subjective level, it feels like what you do to me is more hurtful than what I do to you. But don't be seduced by this kind of thinking. It leads you to say to your partner, "The problems in our relationship are more your fault than mine."

So, what's the solution? It is to recognize that an affair, whatever the circumstances, is the result of a couple being unconscious, meaning they let their reactivity take over. They are still slaves to their emotions, not because they are bad people, but because no one has ever guided them on a path toward consciousness.

We do not know of a better way to grow toward consciousness than to practice regular Dialogues. Nothing trains you better to honor yourself and your discontent than living and practicing the concept that you are worth it. You do deserve a hearing, but you should avoid saying "I deserve it." That only indicates that you don't believe it. Instead, practice the kind of behaviors that give life to those words. Behaviors, not words, are transformative. We often tell clients, "You will be respected to the degree you respect yourself." Your best insurance against your marriage deteriorating is a commitment to keep processing the painful moments. We believe that the more you practice conscious behavior with your partner and other people in your life, the more secure you will become about yourself and the more self-worth you will feel.

We wish you well on your journey of Dialoguing.

∽✦∽

JOKE OF THE DAY

On the way back from a Cub Scouts meeting, my grandson asked my son *the* question. "Dad, I know that babies come from mommies' tummies, but how do they get in there in the first place?" he asked innocently.

After my son hemmed and hawed awhile, my grandson finally spoke up in disgust, saying, "You don't have to make something up, Dad. It's OK if you don't know the answer."

Q&A NUMBER 29

Q: Sometimes I know we should have a Dialogue, but it seems we are feeling worse afterwards. So I just as soon avoid it. Could you comment on this?

A: Good question, one we encounter fairly regularly. To ask for a Dialogue is to risk feeling worse. But let's look at the choices we have.

One is to say nothing and sweep it under the rug. Many of us have tried that strategy, with devastating results. We can keep negative feelings in only for so long. All this negativity builds up and eventually explodes in the worst of ways and at the worst of times. We end up saying things we can never take back and do damage that will take a long time to repair. Keeping in one's negative feelings toward one's partner is also disrespectful of the self, and we often tell clients, "You will be respected to the degree you respect yourself." To say nothing is an invitation for your partner to be abusive toward you.

The second option is to gather your courage and ask for a Formal Dialogue, even though one or both of you may feel worse afterward. The purpose of the Dialogue is twofold: 1) to be heard and hopefully feel understood and validated, and 2) to hear the perspective of the other. Number 2 is where it gets tricky. We all tend to be symbiotic, which means, "I want you to see the world my way, and when you don't, I feel triggered and unsettled." To some degree, we all were raised with a version of, "To love means to clone, and if you love me, you will see, do, and feel the way I do." The Dialogue is a direct challenge to that closely held, albeit unconscious, belief. But the only way to grow and become more conscious is to place ourselves in the position of hearing the perspective of the other, preferably without becoming defensive. And yes, it can be very difficult and painful to be faced with the reality that my partner is not me, thinks so differently from me, and does things in such a weird, illogical way (or at any rate, not how I would do it). That is the pain we have to go through, the surgery before the recovery.

The Formal Dialogue is our ally in moving toward growth and healing. It is an essential part of our journey, the sine qua non of attaining the relationship of our dreams. It is the pain we have to go through to reach the next plateau. Make it a regular ritual in your life so it can help you be curious about your partner and mirror back with empathy what your partner is telling you. Your own inner peace and your dream relationship are waiting for you!

We wish you well on your journey toward breaking the symbiosis.

NOW FOR A BIT OF THEORY

We all want to believe in the beautiful myth that when we fall in love and get married, we will live happily ever after. Because this is such a precious belief, we are convinced that when we encounter conflict in our relationship, we might be with the wrong person. But since Imago theory (see Appendix 2) posits that we marry for the purpose of growth and healing (not happiness, though happiness will be a by-product), we accept from the start that the committed relationship journey will, to some degree, be difficult and painful. You know the saying, "No pain, no gain."

Growth ALWAYS involves pain, so one of our most important sayings is, "Conflict is growth trying to happen." Memorize this saying, burn it into your mind, and develop the courage to face conflict and learn how to constructively work your way through it. The only way to the Promised Land is through the Valley of the Shadow of Death. Your courage will pay off, and it will become easier as you go.

JOKE OF THE DAY

Mary decides to consult a diet doctor.
"What's the most you've ever weighed?" he asks her.
"One hundred fifty-nine pounds."
"And the least?"
"Six pounds, four ounces."

Q&A NUMBER 30

Q: I firmly believe in Imago, even though it didn't work out for my previous relationship. I waited the recommended "at least a year" before pursuing a new relationship. I am now at the beginning stages of a new one and would like to begin to Dialogue to get in the habit, even though we don't have any issues yet because we're still in the "in love" stage. What can we Dialogue about that would set the tone for an emotionally healthy and honest relationship and help keep us in this "in love" phase forever?

A: First, congratulations on waiting for a year. It gives you time to grieve and not be in such an emotionally raw place. Emotions are what cloud our judgment, so there is great wisdom in your willingness to feel the full impact of the pain of the breakup. Many of us want to escape feeling the pain at all costs, but no amount of pretending or covering it up will ease the pain. Facing it gently, lovingly, and respectfully through journaling and/or speaking to a therapist or a good friend—meaning one who will listen without judging either one of you—is how to go through the dark tunnel of breaking up. You not only need to, mourn the person, but you need to mourn the dream you had with that person. So again, congratulations. In a way, waiting a year was the best thing you could have done in preparation for a new relationship.

We hope you thoroughly enjoy the in-love stage you are in. This is a sweet and precious experience in life, but also delicate and fragile. And you know that is true, because of your past experiences.

Now you are right that if the two of you were to have Formal Dialogues, it would set the tone for an emotionally healthy relationship. But would it keep the two of you "in love" forever? No!! The in-love phase is just that, a phase! It is not designed to last. It is designed to bond us together so we can stand side by side, come what may.

Ultimately, our goal in having a committed, intimate relationship is to grow and become a source of healing for each other. But with a new partner, Dialoguing does not make sense. The only thing you can do is to learn to become dialogical. What does that mean? It means that you listen, listen, and listen some more with warmth and empathy and then Mirror not the words or content but the emotions your partner is conveying. This Mirroring can sound something like "Wow, you sound really excited. What an opportunity!" Or it can sound like "You are very angry. That comment was cruel and hurtful to you." Your goal is to get a "yes" from your partner in response.

To become a good dialogical partner, make a commitment to yourself that before you answer, comment on, or react to whatever your partner is saying, you'll hold back (contain), and Mirror your partner's emotions first. Remember, it's not about you, your opinion, or what you would have done in that situation. It's about your partner! Stay focused on your partner. Don't change the subject and start talking about yourself. If you can put your ego aside along with that urge to say how you would have done it, then you will be a safe person for your partner, and then your partner will be able to be honest with you, without fear of being misunderstood, judged, or punished.

As you continue to be a safe person to talk to and share with, your relationship will grow and deepen. You will have built the best foundation possible, one of warmth and compassion. And in time, the feeling of being "in love" will give way to the commitment of "real love." That is our wish for you and for all our faithful readers.

NOW FOR A BIT OF THEORY

Until about two-hundred years ago, marriages were arranged for property, social, and family reasons. But now, here in the West, we have the freedom to choose whom we want to marry, and we do that by surrendering to the "falling in love" process. The urge to get married comes from our urge to grow, heal, and realize our full potential. We all want to maximize our potential, and we instinctively know that it is in relationship where we can accomplish that. Through evolution we fall in love with just the right person: a person who will give us the opportunity to maximize our potential by triggering our unfinished business from childhood, thus giving us the possibility to learn how to handle the situation in a conscious manner.

To weather the storm of growth and healing that will invariably come our way, we can predict with 100% accuracy that the Romantic Love Stage will eventually give way to the Power Struggle Stage, and the greater the level of commitment, the more certain it is that a Power Struggle will ensue.

The way out of the Power Struggle on our way to Real Love is by doing the regular practice of Dialogue together.

❧ ❧

JOKE OF THE DAY

There are three ways to get something done:
do it yourself, hire someone, or forbid your kids to do it.

❧ ❧

Q&A NUMBER 31

Q: When I ask my wife to be less reactive and to change her tone of voice, she always puts it back on me and says she is only reactive because of whatever I've done. How should I deal with this?"

A: Well, good question. We think many of you will identify with it. We hear it quite regularly.

How "should you" deal with this? Let us first remind you not to "should on yourself." *Should*, implies guilt. We make recommendations and suggestions based on the assumption that you want to learn how to handle the situation differently, but not that you should—as if God were going to punish you if you didn't. We don't look for a guilty party. We look at dynamics and personal responsibilities. Also, asking your wife to change her tone is a negative request as well as a judgment of her tone. Our brain is not designed to respond well to negative requests

It's safe to assume your wife does not wake up in the morning deciding, "Hmmmm. I'll have a negative tone of voice today." We assume goodwill in both of you. By far, most human beings (and that includes children) strive to be good, to be the best they can be under the circumstances. But because of emotional wounding, hard as we try, we slip up. It sounds like having a negative tone of voice is one of the ways your wife slips up.

Now the choice of how to deal with her slip-ups is yours. You can respond in a conscious manner or not. The fact that your wife slipped up does not give you the right to slip up as well. But you do have your own frailties, and it is possible that you would answer her slip-ups reactively. We don't want to judge you for having a reactive response, any more than we want to blame your wife. You are just as human and just as fragile as she, but you are also just as responsible as she for the way you respond to her.

So what would a conscious, nonreactive answer be? As always in Imago work, it is to respond to her tone of voice with warmth, empathy, and curiosity. It would sound something like "I can hear some irritation in your voice, and I am guessing I said something that triggered you. Perhaps I inadvertently rubbed a raw nerve and hurt you." At a later time, you want to process what happened. You can't do it now in the midst of churning emotions. It is quite likely that you would find it impossible to Mirror your wife back with kindness and compassion—especially if you feel hurt and judgmental at that moment.

If her tone of voice triggers you at any moment, make the choice to disengage for now. Escalating a fight might feel good in the moment, but it sends the conversation into a downward spiral, and hostile words cannot be taken back. So take a time-out and say, "I'm having a hard time containing right now. I'm going to take a time-out. I'm not abandoning you."

A situation like this requires that you Dialogue about what happened and why you felt triggered. You felt hurt, so it deserves some "unpacking." That really is the beauty and the awesome depth of the Formal Dialogue. When we both feel calmer, we can try to understand in a non-defensive manner the dynamics of the interaction that had so pushed our buttons. Over time, exercising curiosity to help change our behavior has the power to heal and restore connection and wholeness between us.

Happy healing to all!

NOW FOR A BIT OF THEORY

We don't have control over how we feel, but we DO have control over how we act and speak. It takes many years of practice to move away from reactivity and become more conscious in our behaviors.

Understanding Imago theory will not change you. A better understanding of Imago theory may give you the inspiration and energy to "do the practice." Behaviors only change through actual practice. We recommend that you practice some form of Dialoguing several times a week. (See Appendix 1)

⌾⌾

JOKE OF THE DAY

"To do is to be." — Sartre
"To be is to do." — Socrates
"Do be do be do." — Sinatra

⌾⌾

Q&A NUMBER 32

Q: My wife doesn't want to have sex with me. It seems the deal is that I have to be perfect before she is willing to have sex. You have said it is important to ask for what we need, but I don't want her to feel obligated to have sex. Why should I ask if I already know she doesn't want to? I just end up feeling hurt!

A: Another classic question. Why do I have to ask for something when my partner already knows what I want? I don't want to ask my partner to do what she or he doesn't want to do.

At first blush, this seems logical. Yet there is a fault line in this thinking, and that is that somehow committed, intimate relationships should be easy. We think, "My partner should have sex with me spontaneously, the way it used to be. If I have to ask, then it doesn't count, because it will be out of obligation and not love. I don't want her to do it just because I asked. If I have to ask, then it doesn't count."

Yet, that process of asking is exactly what Imago recommends. To love means to love our partner the way our partner needs to be loved. We also need to give our partner a roadmap and guidelines as to what would feel loving to us. This is because if we fell in love, it means we came from very different worlds. It was this complementarity that produced the romantic energy. At the beginning, we experienced this complementarity as "Together, we are whole." Most often, we then gradually experience our differences and the anxiety they arouse in us, and this leads us to make comments such as "I would never do it that way," or "I can't believe you said that!" . . . Ouch!

So first, your partner may not know what exactly you need since your partner's needs are probably the opposite of yours. Second, the goal of intimate relationships is growth and healing, not a stroll down Lovers' Lane. The reason it is difficult for many of us to ask for what we need is that the messages we got during childhood were "You are so selfish! How dare you ask so directly. Who do you think you are?" And we had no choice but to suppress our desire to ask to get our needs met. As we moved into adulthood, the child in us is still very much alive and the internalized message that it was inappropriate for us to be so bold and ask directly for what we need spoke loudly. It's hard to change our internal beliefs. However, the only way to succeed is to start asking directly and positively for what we need, to practice doing the very thing we were told was unacceptable. We have to willingly stretch and courageously face our discomfort. And we have to do it again and again until our psyches begin to let it in that it's OK to ask.

Now there are guidelines to our asking. It's OK to ask, but it's not OK to demand. It's not only OK but essential to ask and stretch into possibly receiving "No, not for now" as a fully acceptable answer. You both need to grow into the "No, not for now" zone. You stretch and ask, and she stretches either by voluntarily giving you this gift or facing the discomfort of saying no and possibly feeling judged. A key word here is *voluntarily*. You don't make your partner do something. Your partner chooses to do or not.

On the other hand, if you never ask, you deny yourself the possibility of feeling loved. And if you never ask, you deny your partner the possibility of growth. And remember, growth for your partner may come from either answer: "Yes," or "No, not for now."

So move ahead and ask for what you need. Both of you can only benefit from it.

NOW FOR A BIT OF THEORY

Since we all want to grow up, become the best we can be, and maximize our potential, nature's best design is that we do this growing up "in relationship." We were born in relationship, we were wounded in relationship, and we grow and heal in relationship. But if we were completely harmoniously compatible in relationship, we would not need to grow and heal. It is the incompatibility that "forces" us to grow up. It is like what they say at the gym: "No pain, no gain." Therefore, nature has designed us to fall in love with an incompatible person who will trigger all our unfinished business from childhood and thus give us the possibility to work it through.

Love, a gift freely given, is what heals. By asking for what we need (Pillar #5 vulnerability – Vol 1 Ch 3), we give our partner the possibility to offer us the gift of love.

❧

JOKE OF THE DAY

Why does E.T. have such big eyes?
Because he saw the phone bill.

❧

Q&A NUMBER 33

Q: I'm an Imago therapist who took your advanced courses recently. I was inspired when you told us about the various rituals you use to help you stay on the Imago journey. I was particularly impressed that you still Dialogue on your morning walks after twenty-five years! Do we ever reach a point where we don't need to dialogue anymore?

A: Well, the answer to that depends on the kind of relationship you want!

Do we ever get so mature that nothing triggers us anymore or that when triggered, we are in such control of our emotions that we are not reactive (either minimizing or maximizing)? This is theoretically possible, but practically, it is not what we observe. We know many older couples and are often saddened by the tone and content of some of their interactions. Many just get used to it and are willing to sweep stuff under the rug. They've had many years of negativity, and either it doesn't seem worth it to them to learn a different way of relating, or they don't believe that it's even possible. So they move into resignation. They may move into parallel relationships so that it is not so painful. She does her thing, he does his.

We feel privileged that we started so long ago, at a time when this work was crucial to keeping our family together. This was such a high motivation to get us on a disciplined approach to our married life. It has been well worth it for us. We believe our children have been the beneficiaries of a calmer, more loving, and less critical environment. And of course, just the fact that our children are doing well buoys us up and motivates us to stay on the journey. Negativity feeds on itself, but so does positivity.

As we get older, we are more and more impacted by the power of early childhood events. The "old language" we learned in childhood becomes the relational language we speak, and learning a new language is difficult at best. The old language has become entwined with our defense system. It is most difficult, terrifying even, to handle our emotions differently, in a "conscious" manner. We have some pretty good role models who function at the individual level, but all hell breaks loose for them when they are in relationship. The noted Buddhist teacher Jack Kornfield was a model guru for many years, teaching all over the world while single, but he informed us that when he came home from India and got married, he had to "start all over again."

The Imago notion that love is loving our partner the way they want to be loved—that is our ultimate growth, that which requires so much of us, that which will lead us to become who we were born to be. And that, dear friends, we believe is a lifelong endeavor, a life of discipline in which we keep validating and honoring the reality, the being, the essence of the other.

We don't know that we will ever get there. But we do believe that the process can be enjoyable and energizing and lead us to a deeply satisfying, examined life.

Happy Dialoguing!

NOW FOR A BIT OF THEORY

All animals are reactive. Being animals, we are reactive. Being human, our journey is to go from reactivity to consciousness. Being conscious, in the way we use it, is a synonym for being loving. Being loving is not being "in love." It is easy to be loving when we are "in love." The definition of "being loving" is "to care for the well-being of someone, borne out in action." Being in love is a feeling. Being loving, or conscious, is an action. It is learning how to love our partner the way he or she wants to be loved. That is difficult to do and indeed a lifelong journey.

JOKE OF THE DAY

How is a hospital gown like insurance?
You're never covered as much as you think you are!

Q&A NUMBER 34

Q: I am afraid to talk about sex with my wife. I have been thinking of having a Formal Dialogue and make a request, but I can't think of SMART requests to get more and better sex. Any suggestions?

A: You are very wise to consider using a Dialogical process to talk about sex. We have often found sex to be a thorny issue. So often, couples have dealt with the problem in angry, accusatory terms that have added layer after layer of anger and hurt. So whatever differences a couple may have in their libidos, the tension has been heightened by criticisms, judgments, and demands, creating an even greater lack of safety and increased frustration. One does not make love if one feels unsafe, angry, resentful, pressured, or ignored. In the animal kingdom, our energies must be free of fear and anxiety before we can feel the life force and sexual energy that are ultimately our birthright. So while sexual issues may have a hormonal component, our experience has been that the biggest component is an emotional one. Learning to Dialogue with each other in a warm, respectful, and validating manner is, from our perspective, the first step.

You want to change the quality of the sexual energy between you. Since you are the one who feels the tension inside (she probably feels it too, but you're the one who wrote the question), we suggest that you initiate a Formal Dialogue (or several) where you simply recognize this is an issue between the two of you and that you, personally, have not handled the situation in a manner you feel proud of. This does not mean she did better than you. But complaining is not a constructive strategy. Look at yourself gently and lovingly and verbalize out loud, within the structure of the Dialogue, how YOU contribute or have contributed to the tension, and let her know that you want to handle the problem differently. Such an approach—self-reflective, proactive, and non-attacking—is the non-negotiable preparation to making progress.

Remember, this has gotten worse over the years not because either one of you is a bad person but because you are both wounded children at heart. Remember that if you could have done better, you would have! Now that you are learning new skills, you can learn to do better—not an easy task, but we think a worthwhile one.

Only after you have accomplished an emotional reconnection do we think you can begin a sexual one. When you make a request, make sure you start with a small one. We have had good success with sensuous massage of one another, first nonsexual and then moving one step at a time toward full sexuality and ending with intercourse, or the equivalent. (This is called "sensate focus" – google it and read the Wikipedia article on it). Begin with once a week at first, or even less. What matters is improvement, not perfection. It may be important that you let her decide when she is ready for whatever next step you would like to take. We have found it helpful for a couple to make a commitment to not having sex for a time and starting with only sensual massages until "the slowest member is ready." If she can trust that you will respect her boundaries, then she can relax and willingly push herself to a new plateau. Feeling respected by you will feel loving and will warm her heart, which will open the door to more satisfying sex.

Thank you for a good question, and our best for the fulfillment of your life energies.

NOW FOR A BIT OF THEORY

The theory session today starts with a short seven-minute video. Go to this URL: http://viewpure.com/MFzDaBzBlL0?ref=bkmk

Being inspired by a lecture or a reading, or even by this video, will not change a thing!! It is the five minutes of practice that he did every day for eight months that made all the difference. The brain is plastic, meaning that it can and will change, but only with frequent and continuous practice! In the video, he says, "Thinking does not equal understanding." We would rather say, thinking or understanding does not bring about change, only <u>practice</u> does!

Learning a language other than our native tongue is very hard (like Bruce's learning to speak French). Criticisms and putdowns, the "native tongue" we learned in childhood will only change after five minutes of practice every day for many months. For this "practice", we recommend couples read their Relationship Vision to each other, and include Appreciations and Intentionalities every day (see Vol 2 Ch 3).

JOKE OF THE DAY

Leaving the party late, two friends compare notes.
"I can never fool my wife," the first says. "I turn off the car engine, coast into the garage, sneak upstairs, and undress in the bathroom. But she always hears me, wakes up, and yells at me for being out late."
"You should do what I do," says his buddy. "I roar into the garage, stomp up the steps, throw open the door, and start kissing my wife. And she pretends to be asleep."

Q&A NUMBER 35

Q: Our work schedules make it so we hardly ever see each other, but we need the income. Is there any solution to this?

A: You are in a difficult situation, to be sure. And it is entirely possible that your current situation does not have a satisfying solution. We wish we could always come up with feel-good possibilities. Sometimes, because "life happens," those good or satisfying possibilities are evasive.

So what are your choices? Well, one thing that comes to mind is that even though you may have to surrender to what is, simultaneously, keep on your search to see if anything can be changed. Accept that which you cannot change, yet remain proactive, keeping an open mind to changes that could actually happen. Sometimes we fall into a defeatist slump that keeps us somewhat depressed and discouraged and blocks us from thinking outside the box. While we recognize that it is a tenuous balance to maintain, being fully accepting of our life as it is today yet continuing to search and think outside the box is a dynamic we want to keep alive. Life is fluid. Situations change. We grow and mature, and so do our kids.

If we can remain fully alive and expect the best of life, life often rewards us. The pitfall we want to avoid is that of feeling sorry for ourselves, that of feeling like a victim. So, now, let's assume that you have explored all possibilities and are totally confident that this current situation is not an escape from intimacy and vulnerability with each other. Here are a few suggestions.

Make those precious few moments you have with each other count. Ideally once a month and no less than every other month, take a weekend off together, just the two of you. It doesn't have to be far away from your normal environment, but put some distance between you and it. Make sure you leave the children and pets behind in good hands. Spend at least one night away and focus on each other. Do not become tourists, become lovers. Hold hands, walk, look into each other's eyes, and tell each other how fortunate you are to have the jobs you do have, to be in each other's lives, to be alive, to feel each other's touch, and to be on life's journey together.

Focus on thanking your partner and finding all sorts of little things your partner does for you and your family. Hopefully, you have a relationship vision (if you don't, take the time to create one—see Volume Two Chapter 3). Read it out loud to each other.

Make time also for a sexual connection. This is a time to celebrate each other in all human realms: physical, sexual, emotional and spiritual. Let your hearts be warmed by the present moment even though all is not as you might wish it to be. But make the choice to accept the present situation fully in order to be wholeheartedly present for each other.

Our best to you both.

≈

JOKE OF THE DAY

René Descartes was in a bar. At last call, the bartender asked him if he'd like another drink.
Descartes said, "I think not."
And he disappeared.

≈

Q&A NUMBER 36

Q: My partner clearly remembers feeling hurt as a child, but I don't. You say that we were equally wounded. My parents were really good people and I received very little wounding. How do you explain that?"

A: Good question! We identify a lot with this question because it parallels our own dynamics. We have no doubt that your parents were good people, but neither do we doubt that your partner's parents were good people as well.

Let's all remember that at heart, we are all good people and that good people make mistakes too. We do, we did with our parenting, and our parents do and did, and so do our children. We make mistakes because we don't know any better, and sometimes we know better but can't control our emotions. If a wound is too deep and too raw, it is very difficult to be intentional in the moment. What we call containment in Imago therapy is a very difficult state to reach and a task that requires a lot of skill. It requires much consistent practice, bolstered by a desire and a commitment to be intentional in the way we relate to others—especially to our intimate partner.

The Imago theory postulates that if we fell in love with each other and decided to move in together, we were roughly equally wounded and we now contribute equally to the tension in the relationship. What is predictable is that one of us tends to deal with pain by retreating (moving away from the terror of emotional intimacy) while the other is terrified of aloneness and of feeling abandoned. Both feel unworthy of being loved, and both hurt the other equally in the unconscious manner in which they reactively protect themselves. One is not better than the other.

There are several reasons why a person may not remember their childhood wounding. The first is that forgetting is actually one of our protective mechanisms. Our psyches are fragile, and we caution against hypnosis because it may break through that protection too quickly, before we are ready to face the truth consciously.

Another reason is that when we were children, it was very important that we exonerated our parents. If our parents were inappropriate in any way, meaning verbally or physically abusive, we justified their behaviors by telling ourselves we deserved it. We told ourselves, *This punishment is for my own good.* We believed that, because we dared not counter Mom and/or Dad. Our survival depended on our relationship with them. We could not take the risk of displeasing or disagreeing with them. As children, that was the trap we were in: if we became an independent self, we ran the risk of displeasing our parents and cutting off our lifeline. Teenagers are willing to take that risk, but not younger children.

The last reason we don't remember our hurts from childhood is that many of those hurts took place during the first three years of life, when we were most demanding of our parents' focused attention. We needed their unconditional and reliable emotional availability. When we didn't get it, the pain was stored in our body and our primitive brain. Because we didn't have access to language, those memories could not be consolidated in a manner that would help us make sense of our own history in order to create a coherent narrative.

But there is good news. We can gain access to those long-forgotten and never consolidated memories by focusing on what frustrates us in others, especially what frustrates us in our intimate partner. That is our best window into our own psyche. By lovingly working through the frustration you experience with your partner, you will begin to bring healing to those long-forgotten hurts that, as long as they remain unhealed, dominate and run your life (albeit unconsciously). Those childhood wounds are relentless in their demands to be dealt with and transformed into constructive energy.

Keep doing the Dialogical work together, keep working through your frustrations with one another, and you both will gradually become aware how you are equally wounded

We wish you well on your journey to consciousness.

JOKE OF THE DAY

Servers at Disney World's Cinderella Castle treat you like royalty—literally. After lunch, our waiter asked, "Is there anything else My Lord wishes?"
"Yes," I joked. "I'd like my wife to treat me like this at home."
He bowed to my wife. "My Lord desires to be treated like a king in his castle. What is My Lady's answer?"
She said, "He's spent a little too much time in Fantasyland."

Q&A NUMBER 37

Q: I want to have Dialogues with my partner, but she usually hammers on me during Dialogues—and then she becomes frustrated with me because I say no to more Dialogues. Isn't it OK for me to refuse Dialogues? We both feel stuck!

A: You are describing a classic scenario. We know many couples will identify with you. On the other hand, many of us have experienced the power of the Formal Dialogue and we do believe that you would benefit from it—but it is hard to pull off at home, without a coach. This shows us the grip emotions have on us: we are driven by our limbic brains! And that is our journey: to master our emotions enough so that we can regain our balance, our reasonable selves and relate to each other in a conscious manner. Our Imago theory postulates that Dialoguing with our partner is one powerful way to get there. There seems to be a direct correlation between the importance and centrality of mastering our emotions and the difficulty of attaining a calm groundedness.

We are convinced that it is the regular practice of the Dialogue, Mirroring EVERY word that comes out of your partner's mouth and Validating your partner's perspective, that will break the emotional symbiosis. If you and your partner Mirror each other's every word, you will provide safety for each other, in that you will become 100% predictable (review Chapter 1), and safety is the non-negotiable precondition to bringing healing to your relationship.

So what might be helpful for the two of you on that journey?

1. Start by deciding together on a regular time during the week to Dialogue—no less than once a week, but twice if at all possible. Trying to Dialogue in the midst of an emotional breakdown is counterproductive, so Dialogue by the calendar, not by the emotions!

2. Make an agreement that you will both respect the time-out signal. Make sure to stay away from making accusations, such as "There you go again. You're hammering me." That is a sure way to pour fuel on the fire of negativity. Instead, say, "I am having a hard time containing right now and I am going to take a time-out. Use your hand signal as you say that, and walk away. Containing just enough to say that sentence is a huge step on the road to becoming intentional.

3. At first, the two of you might want to alternate asking for the Dialogue, although we mostly prefer that one partner asks another based on a personal experience of some unfinished business. But what if you don't have any unfinished business? Then Dialogue about something positive: a movie you just saw, a book you are reading, or your plans for vacationing this year. You can always tell your partner "Let me share with you some of the ways you have enriched my life."

4. Another guideline we find important is to rigidly (yes, rigidly!) limit any send to ten minutes. Both of you will feel safer this way. You both know what you're saying yes to, and it already has boundaries. And no, you will not unpack everything in a twenty-minute Dialogue, but Dialoguing is a way of life, which includes containment. So we chip away a bit during any single Dialogue and may have to continue next time. At least you are on the journey toward consciousness because you are practicing both Dialoguing and containment.

We wish you well on your road to intentionality.

JOKE OF THE DAY

Waiter: "And how did you find your steak sir?"
Diner: "Well, I just pushed aside the pea and there it was . . ."

Q&A NUMBER 38

Q: Yesterday, my wife wanted me to Validate her. How do I Validate her when I totally disagree with her viewpoint?

A: This is a question many of us have bumped into. Here are some of our thoughts.

You probably have heard us say, "Validation is not agreement!" It isn't, but let's unpack that a bit. During the initial interview, on the first day we ever meet a couple, we introduce them to the concept of validation by showing them a coaster, one side of which is made of cork and the other of marble. We have each partner look at the coaster from a different side, describe what they see, and say to each other, "Wow, I had no idea." And of course, the reason is that they see the object so totally differently.

When I validate you, I recognize what a past event was like for you and that you felt hurt, surprised, broadsided, or neglected. By validating what it's like to be you, I recognize you as a human being, separate from me and with intrinsic worth. I am working on letting that in, on being impacted by your telling me what your experience was. I may have had a totally different recollection or experience, but I am working on getting what it was like for you. I transcend my ego and move out of myself to focus on you. Doing that, is obviously a very difficult endeavor, but very, very worthwhile. It is a process and a journey toward peace.

During Validation, we like using the words, "Your perspective is important and valuable to me, and you make sense." We don't let our couples analyze why the other makes sense. You make sense because you just told me what it was like to be you. So in order to make progress in the Validation process, the couple must be willing to step beyond ideas of "right or wrong" or "what really happened." Unless we have a video recording of what happened, we'll never know for sure the objective reality. And even then, there might be different interpretations of the event. What is important, however, is the emotional imprint left behind. We know what we felt—that is non-arguable. That being said, it is helpful to know what the words were that carried a charge. Or was it the situation? Was it too public? Did it happen in front of your parents or the children? Before we can get into the nitty-gritty of a painful interaction, we need to feel taken seriously, to feel that our experience is valuable and honored by the other, not put down or dismissed. Instead, we want to develop a spirit of loving and kind curiosity, not by asking questions (questions put us on the defensive) but through accurate Mirroring in a warm and accepting tone. Try to practice with a movie or a show you both experienced differently, a piece of music, or a different political point of view or spiritual discipline.

So Validate your wife. Validate her even though you have a different perspective. Validate, Validate, Validate. Your relationship can only blossom from it.

We wish you well on your road toward consciousness.

NOW FOR A BIT OF THEORY
We see Validation as one of the BIGGEST growth journeys that any couple has to make. Validating your partner is the only way to break the symbiosis that is at the heart of ALL problems with couples. Being symbiotic is the reason why couples fight. Being symbiotic is saying, "I want you to see the world MY way. I want you to think, believe, and feel the way I do."

Learning to validate requires practice. Hearing an inspiring lecture on how everyone sees the world differently from each other will not do the trick. You actually have to say, "Your perspective on this is important and valuable to me, and you make sense."

When your wife says, "You disregard me and never validate me," you need to say, "Your perspective on this is important and valuable to me, and you make sense."

When your husband says, "Watching football and baseball are important grounding activities for me," you need to say, "Your perspective on this is important and valuable to me, and you make sense."

When your adult son says, "I do pot because it gives me unique spiritual insights," you need to say, "Your perspective on this is important and valuable to me, and you make sense."

When your mother says, "You don't love me anymore because you never call," you need to say, "Your perspective on this is important and valuable to me, and you make sense."

Eventually, you will be able to let go of the feeling that your way of thinking, believing, and seeing the world is the only right way, and you will be able to let your partner be himself or herself in your presence. When this happens, differentiation has taken place—and the goal of good, healthy relationships is to be differentiated enough to be able to validate others while at the same time holding on to your boundaries with warmth and grace.

∽⌒∼

JOKE OF THE DAY

Fresh out of gift ideas, a man buys his mother-in-law a large plot in an expensive cemetery. On her next birthday, he buys her nothing, and she demands to know why.

He says, "You still haven't used the present I gave you last year."

∽⌒∼

Q&A NUMBER 39

Q: How long does Imago therapy take? We've been at this for eight months. I see on the Internet that this is a ten-week program for many couples. Why are we different?

A: Many people ask this question, and the answers are as varied as there are couples practicing Imago work.

Let us first respond to the notion that Imago is a ten-week program for many couples. In our twenty-five years of practice, we have never seen that happen. In our experience, Formal Dialogues in their various forms are most successful when used regularly, over time. There is no Shazam! just a regular, steady practice of really hearing the perspective of the other and learning to ask for what we need in a direct manner, behaviorally and positively. This alone takes time for most of us. But every couple moves at a different rate.

We (Bruce and Francine) have been practicing since October 1989. For the first ten or fifteen years, not a day went by that we didn't Dialogue. Francine remembers having a long list of topics in her head (since it is only one topic per Dialogue). Now, we still take our daily walks, but we Dialogue maybe two times a week. It's not nearly as heated as it once was, but we like to use the Dialogue for topics we think may have a degree of controversy. We both agree that we listen to the other better when we place ourselves within the containment of the Dialogue.

To give you other reference points, we have been running Imago Couples' Therapy Groups for at least twenty years. They are relatively inexpensive and only held every other week. Participating in these groups is a gentle way to stay on the path with like-minded couples. One couple has been coming for over ten years! They don't plan on quitting. It has been their "relational hygiene." Other couples have been coming to group for five or eight years. Some are brand-new. Couples stay as long as it feeds them spiritually. Before a couple stops coming to group, we like them to be able to Dialogue totally on their own without our having to intervene or coach them in any way. That means that they have learned to send in a manner that shares their experience without accusing their partner. It means they can own what their contribution is in any particular situation and can state what they wish they would have done differently, without judgment toward self or the other.

By far, the biggest problem we see working with couples is that they quit too soon. Some never come back and some come back later in tears. Other factors we see as important are how much a couple practices on their own and how much healing they need from their childhood. It also depends on their commitment to a conscious relationship and to their personal growth, rather than focusing on their partners.

A big problem we see occurs when members of a couple go to their individual therapist. An individual therapist is usually not concerned with the dynamics of the relationship and often undermines them. They often collude with the client and see the partner as holding them back from freedom and maximizing their potential. Of course, it is possible that the individual therapist is lovingly bringing the client to personal responsibility and does not let the client talk negatively about the partner. But in our experience, that is a rare event. Often, the therapist and the client don't believe in equal contribution to the disruption in the relationship.

We are currently reading a wonderful book: Insight Dialogue, by Greg Kramer, who comes from the Buddhist tradition. He poignantly separates intrapersonal and interpersonal meditation. He shares his own experience, in which he used to practice only intrapersonal meditation (even if in a room with other people) only to face renewed tension with his partner. All the inner peace and groundedness were gone in a second. So he advocates interpersonal meditation as a spiritual practice. The more we read his book, the more we see Formal Dialoguing as just that: an interpersonal spiritual practice where we surrender our Ego and totally focus on our partner's words. It leaves us with no defensiveness and no hunger (the Buddha's term), just a growing compassion for the other and yourself in your pain and struggle, trying to keep those in balance and making the best decisions that will honor self and other.

Participating in Imago sessions constitutes the "training wheels" until you can Dialogue on your own. While eight months feels like a long time, in the larger scheme of things, it is very little. Stay with it as long as you think it positively impacts your life. Don't stay in Imago work out of guilt. Give it your best as honestly as you can and be prepared to surrender and let go.

As for the spiritual journey itself, we hope it is and will continue to be an intimate and integral part of your daily life.

NOW FOR A BIT OF THEORY

Wade Luquet wrote a book called, *Short-Term Couples Therapy: The Imago Model in Action*. This is what you probably saw on the Internet. It is an excellent book written in response to the fact that many insurance programs often only give ten couples therapy sessions to clients. This book is an outline of what therapists can do in ten sessions so that couples will get a good introduction to Imago therapy quickly. But Imago therapy is a practice, not an insight to be learned. Insight and learning will not change your marriage. When you enter Imago therapy, you are entering a lifetime journey of moving from reactivity to intentionality, from unconsciousness to consciousness.

Say you asked a Christian minister, "How long will I need to attend church?" He would respond, "Our recommendation is that it be a lifelong practice." Or say you asked a Buddhist master, "How long will I need to do meditation?" He would say, "Our recommendation is that it be a lifelong practice." So how long do you need to practice Formal Dialogues? Our recommendation is that it be a lifelong practice.

We wish you well on your journey toward consciousness.

JOKE OF THE DAY

Asked about the kind of job he wanted, an applicant stated, "I seek full authority but limited responsibility."

Q&A NUMBER 40

Q: When I ask for a time-out, it makes things worse. My wife gets angry and won't stop. So that technique does not work for us. What can we do instead?

A: Yes, on paper, asking for a time-out looks simple. But the actual execution can be tricky. In couplehood, landmines are everywhere, so the two of you need to talk when you are both feeling good about each other and decide whether asking for a time-out is a technique you are both willing to embrace. Check that you are both willing to make a commitment to respect the time-out. Now that doesn't mean that your primitive brain won't act out, but it means that you are now enrolling your logical, reasonable brain. That is a solid foundation, even though it offers no guarantee that either one of you won't break out of the process.

So what next? Here are a few pointers.

First, when you ask for a time-out, make sure to do so without accusing your partner of anything. Clearly state, "I am having a hard time right now. I am going to take a time-out." During your initial meeting, when you both agree on some guidelines, agree that you are both committed to completing the Dialogue later. The time-out is a stop-gap measure to stop the bleeding, so to speak. It is important that you both know asking for a time-out is not a way of avoiding Dialogues. Whoever initiated the Dialogue will need to be the one to pick it up later, when you are both calmer and better able to listen and be present.

A second guideline is to make sure neither one of you coaches the other. That is usually a trigger and a source of much anger.

Lastly, while it is very tempting to want the other to behave differently, the ball is in YOUR court for YOU to behave differently. That is the crux of the work. Part of your ground rules are that you will leave the room or even the house if the other does not respect the request for time-out (if you leave the house, tell her where you are going and when you will be back—and be true to your word). There is no judgment in this, only compassion that you both are having a hard time containing right now. But by all means, don't sit there and listen to your partner berate you. Don't judge her, only understand that she is having a meltdown. Have compassion for her and yourself as well and leave the situation without opening your mouth. Whatever you might say at the moment will only fuel the fire, so become the change you want to see in her. You would like to be treated with respect, so treat yourself with respect. Also, don't think in terms of punishment for your partner's harsh words. Punishment does not work, but clear boundaries that you enact do work. Also, there should be no words during a time-out. The words have to be said in your initial Dialogue, when the two of you decide how to handle a heated situation and a time-out. In the current situation, only behaviors are needed—behaviors that say, "This is my boundary, which I set to be respectful to myself and not lash out at you."

This is one of those situations where behaviors speak louder than words. If you change YOUR behavior, it will change the dynamics of the relationship. So we recommend you put all your energy into learning to set your boundaries kindly yet firmly. Then and only then can you expect miracles.

NOW FOR A BIT OF THEORY

Pia Mellody says that boundaries are at the heart of all relationship problems. We say in Imago that the goal of good Dialoguing is connection and differentiation. Connection is not enmeshment, and differentiation is not emotional distance. There cannot be connection without differentiation, and there cannot be differentiation without holding boundaries.

Holding boundaries is very difficult. To make it easier, we often get angry and shout "No!" But that is not boundary setting. That is acting out our state of disempowerment. One of the reasons holding boundaries is so hard is because it always risks the relationship. Your partner says, "Change!" and when you do change, you upset the equilibrium in your relationship, so your partner says, "Change back!" Yet, we believe holding boundaries is an essential condition for positive change in any relationship.

We need to learn the most difficult task of all, that of holding boundaries with warmth AND firmness. Having made agreements ahead of time about how to manage time-outs, when you do call time-out, this is not the time to stop and listen, this is the time to remain quiet and get up and leave the room.

We wish you well on your journey toward conscious living.

❦

JOKE OF THE DAY

A man on a bicycle approached the US border from Mexico. He was carrying a heavy sack. "What's in the sack?" asked the border guard. "Sand," came the reply.

The guard checked, and sure enough it was sand. So he let the man through.

A week later, the man on the bicycle appeared again, carrying a heavy sack.

"What's in the sack?" asked the border guard. "Sand."

The guard checked, verified that it was sand, and let the cyclist through.

This continued on a weekly basis for six months until one day, the cyclist with the sack full of sand failed to show up. A few days later, the guard chanced upon the man in a downtown bar.

"Hey," said the guard. "You've been driving us crazy for the past six months. We're damn sure you were smuggling something through. In strictest confidence, tell me what it was."

"Bicycles," replied the man.

Q&A NUMBER 41

Q: My wife feels accused so easily. I'd rather text her than talk to her. Is it possible for one to be too sensitive, or is it always my fault?

A: We sense your frustration and discouragement. Learning to love and grow intimate relationships stretches us in every direction and demands so much of us that we sometimes wonder if it's worth all the trouble. But a part of you "knows" it's worth it, and that's why you've written us with your question.

Let's start with the easy part: No, it's not always your fault—nor hers, for that matter. You always both contribute to the tension. Nonetheless, the only worthwhile endeavor is to ask yourself, "How did I contribute to this particular conflict?" Without an outside objective observer, answering this question may be close to impossible. After all, we are all doing our best, and if we knew how to do it better, we would. We are all doing our best with the strength and knowledge we have at the moment.

Let us share with you some of our observations over the past 25+ years that we have been working with couples. There is a trend that negatively impacts relationships. It is captured in the following seemingly unrelated statements:

- "You never try to please me."
- "You're always late for things that are important to me."
- "You're too scared to stand up for yourself."
- "Are you kidding? You're the most valuable employee they have."
- "You are such a good cook, you should go ahead and prepare a banquet for our friends."

All these statements share one thing in common: They are an analysis of your partner's character (negative or positive), and as such, they increase your partner's defensiveness. They may therefore cause you to declare your partner "too sensitive." Our recommendation is to think in these terms instead: "Yes, my partner is sensitive, and that's because she is a wounded child. So how can I be a source of healing rather than an irritant to her wound? I have touched a raw nerve of my partner's, and I want to learn what I said or did that caused her reaction. I want to learn a different and better way to relate to her."

The reason we tend to analyze the other is because we are afraid of being vulnerable. When we were vulnerable as children, we paid a painful price. We don't want to repeat the mistakes of our past, so we unconsciously close the door of vulnerability and focus instead on making an analysis of the other. In this way, we keep the focus away from ourselves. That feels safer—but it destroys relationships! One analysis after the other will erode the love and goodwill that enlivened us at the beginning of our relationship.

We want to use this opportunity to encourage all of you to start a journey of greater vulnerability with your partner (Pillar #5 – see Volume One Chapter 3). This requires a huge leap of faith, as our gut reaction is to think, I'll never be good enough if I reveal who I really am. The rewards of taking that leap will match the fears it replaced and the courage it took to risk rejection.

We wish you well on your journey toward vulnerability.

JOKE OF THE DAY

Imaginary new condom brands and their slogans:
Nike condoms: Just do it.
Toyota condoms: Oh...oh, what a feeling!
Pringles condoms: Once you pop, you can't stop.

KFC condoms: Finger-lickin' good.
Ford condoms: The best never rest.
Bounty condoms: The quicker picker-upper.
Energizer condoms: It keeps going and going and going.
M&M's condoms: It melts in your mouth, not in your hand.
Star Trek condoms: To boldly go where no man has gone before.

NUMBER 42

For last "Q&A" we want to say the following:

We believe that an important element to getting the relationship of your dream is the quality of your listening. The following reading has touched us deeply and we want to share it with you.

LISTENING WITH YOUR HEART

Real love listens, knowing that it is in the mystery of exchange that we are bonded and that such an exchange occurs not only through what is said but through what is profoundly received. Speaking is done through the mouth, but listening is done with the heart—where meanings sink in like a stone in a pond, leaving an imprint at the deepest level.

Take the opportunity of this day to really listen to someone close to you. For while we may be relieved when we speak—delivered of the burden of information or feelings that we have been carrying in solitude—we are transformed when we listen.

The stone that falls to the bottom of the pond when we listen impinges on our souls, requiring that we make room in our hearts to feel the imprint of the essence of another human being.

Daphne Rose Kingma, "A Garland of Love" (November 25)

What a wonderful and energizing challenge to look forward to in this coming year: not listening with our defenses up and our ammunition at the ready, not trapping our partner in some old and painful behavior from him or her or our family of origin, but opening our heart to let in the knowledge that our partner is a wonderful human being (after all, we married him or her, deep hurts and all), and learning to make room in our hearts so we feel the imprint of the essence of our partner. What a vision!

But how do we get there? You already know the answer! We listen and listen and listen some more, we warmly Mirror and Mirror again, and we Validate—telling each other that we do make sense. We stretch into seeing a different perspective, and we tell each other that that perspective is worthwhile and that we want to let ourselves be enriched by that different perspective. We ask ourselves the questions, painful as they are, "What's my part in this conflict? What's my 50-percent contribution? Am I willing to change that?"

That's how we listen with our hearts.

Happy listening!

NOW FOR A BIT OF THEORY

At the Annual Imago Conference in 2013, Harville gave a great lecture about what Freud REALLY was doing when he performed psychoanalysis. Freud called it *Talking Therapy*, but as Harville analyzed what really went on in those sessions on the couch, he realized Freud's success resulted from the fact that Freud was really doing *Listening Therapy*. Freud was a great listener, and that made all the difference. His analysis and interpretations were often aggressive, but his listening was magical and very healing.

We all yearn to be listened to!

ᢙᡐ᳑ᢙ

JOKE OF THE DAY

Have you heard the latest scandal? Dr. Pepper was drunk at a party.

ᢙᡐ᳑ᢙ

INDEX TO THE 42 QUESTIONS AND ANSWERS

After reading all 42 questions and answers, you may want to review some of the Q&As based on the topics raised. This index will help you find the Q&As that addresses your concern.

3

Making Requests Designed To Get Your Needs Met

While some of us speak English fluently and effortlessly, others of us have a different mother tongue and had to invest time and effort to learn English. But, learn English we did. We did it well enough that people understand us, although, as we like to tell our clients, we keep our accent – at least some.

Something similar happened in our relational skills. We learned a "relationship language" from our parents. That's the relational language we speak spontaneously, and with natural fluency. Sadly, it is primarily centered around criticisms. "You never... You always... Why did you... I can't believe you said... I think that looks horrible... and on and on. The problem is that when our partner hears our criticisms, his or her old brain experiences us as an enemy. We love each other and yet we experience the other as a threat to our survival. Illogical to be sure, but do not look for logic in our old brain. Let's learn instead how to work with it and its lack of logic. One road to recovery from our "relational language of origin" is to learn to handle frustrations in our current relationship by making requests that would alleviate those frustrations. These requests need to be for an observable behavior, asked in a positive manner, and for a limited period of time: a small step in the direction we want to go.

"You're trying to control me."
"You're not interested in my opinion."
"You couldn't care less about how or what I feel."
"You never try to please me."
" You always put me down."

Ouch!... Those statements hurt. They are reactive and put salt on raw wounds. We believe they can only lead to more hurt and more disconnection.

So, what do we recommend you do instead?

As mentioned in our Pillar #1 and #4 (see Volume One Chapter 3), when in doubt, absolutely assume that your partner has good intentions and move into vulnerability regarding yourself and curiosity about the other, rather than an analysis of the intentions of your partner.

Here are the steps we recommend:

1. Share your hurt in a Formal Dialogue to deepen your feelings associated with the circumstances around any one of these statements.
2. Get in touch with a need you have that is not currently being met, and is expressed in any of the above statements. For example, "I need to feel taken seriously by you." and
3. Make a request.

When making a request, there are several aspects to be mindful of. Here are three possible requests that most likely would not be effective:

"It would be great if we could eat earlier."
"I'd like you to be warmer and more affectionate."
"I'd like you to come home on time."

Why are we saying that these requests will most likely not produce the desired effect? Because they are vague, tentative, open ended and not behaviorally grounded.

Also, don't make a request that a dead person could do, for example:

"Don't yell at me."
"Don't be so emotional."
"Don't bite your finger nails."

A dead person could do all these things! The problem here is that the requests are worded negatively and that our brains do not respond well to negative requests.

Here is an example of a request that meets the requirements for being a what we call a SMART request: "Because of my meetings on Wednesday nights, I would like to sit down to dinner at 5:45 p.m. Would you be willing to have dinner ready by then for the next two weeks?"

Here is how this is a SMART request. It is:

S – Specific   (Wednesday nights at 5:45 pm)
M – Measureable   (Every Wednesday at 5:45 pm)
A – Attainable   (Small shift in timing)
R – Relavant to the frustration or the need
T – Time limited   (For the next two weeks)

The person making the request will then ask the partner to write down the request and rate it. The rating goes as follows: E for easy, C for challenging or N, not for now. We have a form we like to use and here is what it looks like.

In the form below, the person has made two requests:

Sample Request List

I, _____George_____ (insert name), want to stretch and give you,
_____Mary___ (insert name), the following gifts as an expression of my
care and love. Stretching is needed, but I am willing to work hard at it.

Rate the request as E for "Easy", C for "Challenging," or N for
"Not for Now."

Date of Request	Gift to be Given	Rating E, C, or N	Date Gift Reviewed Write positive comments only
Sep 28, '17	I would like you to have dinner ready by 5:45 p.m for the next two weeks.	C	
Oct 1, '17	When you get home from work, I would like you to look me up in the house and give me a 3 sec hug and say, "I love you" three times this week.	E	
Need Statement: I need to feel taken seriously by you			

Notice that if the requests are granted (E or C), they are gifts of
love. It is the discipline of learning to love our partner the way our
partner needs to be loved.

THE IMPORTANCE OF REGULAR REVIEWS

Changes in behaviors are very difficult to achieve and equally difficult to sustain. Despite much goodwill between partners and their desire to please one another, we have found a very strong tendency to revert to previous behaviors or even never implement the request to begin with. The integration of new behaviors is a slow and laborious process. But a relationship will not improve if there are no changes in behavior! Insight alone doesn't change anything. Because of that, we recommend having a formal "Request Review" every two weeks. This will help keep you on top of this very important aspect of your work. We suggest that most requests be for only one or two weeks. The purpose of the review is for feedback and tweaking the request if necessary in order to really meet the needs of the "requester". Make sure you don't shame your partner. Leave the "punitive parent" behind and approach the review from a spirit of loving kindness, believing that your partner has goodwill but is also fully human and therefore prone to slip-ups and forgetfulness. That is human nature. Integrating new behaviors into our repertoire is truly difficult. If we approach the review of Requests from a critical place, the chances are very great that we will not succeed. So make every effort to approach your partner in a spirit of curiosity. You may be disappointed and maybe even upset if your partner did not do the request, but make sure you are also curious about what's going on for him or her because you choose to believe in your partner's goodwill.

It would also be very beneficial for you to reflect on the question, "Is there something I am doing that contributes to my own failure, something I do that sabotages my requests?" We have talked about our fear of intimacy. We both want it, and then we do the very things that will ensure that we remain disconnected and alone. We will be tempted to blame our partner for not being warm and loving and compassionate, but we forget to look at our own prickly behaviors.

Relationships will not change unless behaviors change, and it only takes one partner to change to bring about a shift in the dynamics of the relationship. Yes, it is painfully difficult and slow, and it taxes us in unbelievable ways, still, don't wait for your partner to change. Instead, become the change you want to see in your partner. For example, if you want to feel more appreciated, begin by appreciating him or her more than you currently do. If you want your partner to be a person of his/her word, hold yourself accountable with your own words. If you want more respect, be more respectful of the other.

Because we believe that structure brings about safety, we recommend you review requests using the following outline:

INSTRUCTIONS FOR THE REVIEW OF BEHAVIOR REQUESTS

1. Choose a time and place where you won't be disturbed. This should be a regular ritual that you both commit to.
2. The person working on a new behavior which we will refer to as partner 1, starts by reading the request that had been made by partner 2: "You asked that I . . ." Partner 1 then looks at partner 2 and asks, "How did I do on that?" If s/he did well, s/he gives the list to partner 2 to make a comment in the right-hand column, such as "I liked it," "Great", "I'm appreciative", "Thank you!", a smiley face, etc. Initial and date the comment. If the behavior was not done, leave the space blank. Don't write negative comments.
3. Partner 1 then asks, "Is this still important to you?" After the answer, s/he will ask, "What would you like to do with this request?" Partner 2 can decide to keep the request as is, make a small amendment, or eliminate it. If partner 1 decides to continue granting that request s/he will indicate that by crossing out

the old date and putting the new date in the left-hand column. Partner 1 may also want to re-rate the request. Sometimes after living with a request for a couple of weeks, a person may realize it was harder or easier than initially thought, and may choose to change the rating from easy (E) to challenging (C), or even "not for now" (N).

4. Dialogue about the requests not done, including requests marked as N (not for now). Explore the pain and fears behind not being able to grant or do the request at this time.

We have found that Request Reviews, like Formal Dialogues, need to be calendar driven, not feelings driven, done out of commitment to the process and not based on the emotions of the moment.

After a review, your list might look like this:

Reviewed and Changed Sample Request List

I, _____George_____ (insert name), want to stretch and give you, _____Mary_____ (insert name), the following gifts as an expression of my care and love. Stretching is needed, but I am willing to work hard at it.

Rate the request as E for "Easy", C for "Challenging," or N for "Not for Now."

Date of Request	Gift to be Given	Rating E, C, or N	Date Gift Reviewed Write positive comments only
~~Sep 28, '17~~ Oct 14, '17	I would like you to have dinner ready by 5:45 p.m for the next two weeks?	~~C~~ E	Oct 14, '17 Great. Loved it :-)
~~Oct 1, '17~~ Oct 14,'17	When you get home from work, I would like you to look me up in the house and give me a 3 sec hug and say, "I love you" ~~three times this week.~~ two times this week.	~~E~~ C	Oct 14, 17 I loved it! :-) Thank you.

Need Statement: I need to feel loved and taken seriously by you

We have included here a blank copy of the **Request List** so that you can make copies.

Request List

I, _____ (insert name), want to stretch and give you, _____(insert name), the following gifts as an expression of my care and love. Stretching is needed, but I am willing to work hard at it.

Rate the request as E for "Easy" to do, C for "Challenging," or N for "Not for Now."

Date of Request	Gift to be Given	Rating E, C, or N	Date Gift Reviewed Write positive comments only
Need Statement:			

Epilogue

Well, we have come to the end of our time together.
We trust that some ideas have grabbed you and that you will be motivated to invest the time necessary to nurture your intimate partnership. Relationships are precious – they are as precious as they are fragile. They buoy us to great highs and to deep lows. We always know when a person has fallen in love. We see it in their step. We hear it in their voice. We observe it in their energy and we see the joy captured in their smile.

We hope you will learn to listen to each other with your heart – to listen with deep appreciation for your partner and with a renewed commitment to learn to love each other the way the other needs to be loved.

You are worth it!

Your relationship is worth it!

The steps we have outlined in this trilogy of three volumes, if you are willing to follow them, will absolutely lead you to the relationship of your dreams.

Appendix 1

The Formal Dialogue and a Step-by-Step Guide

Here we lay out what a Formal Dialogue might look like, followed by our check sheet.

There are two participants in a Formal Dialogue: the sender and the receiver. They change roles during the Dialogue at which point the initial sender becomes the receiver. It consists of four stages: Mirroring, Validation, Empathy, and Response.

1) **Mirroring:** The person who feels unsettled and wants to process what happened, makes an appointment: *"I would like to have a Formal Dialogue. Is this a good time for you?"* That person is now the initial sender. This serves the purpose of keeping them safe and is the first step to relate to each other respectfully about a potentially touchy subject. The sender speaks about a specific event and shares the inner experience regarding that event: *"I felt devastated when you said . . . in front of my colleague. Even now I still feel hurt and angry."* When you share your feelings, be especially careful to stay away from criticism, shame, blame or analyzing your partner negatively, such as, "You're always so insensitive..." "You enjoy shaming me in

public... even in private for that matter." Under the energy of anger, it is easy to attack the other.

Another example might be: *"I would like to talk about yesterday when you arrived late for dinner. I got worried that you had forgotten our date night, and then I felt stood up and unimportant."* The receiver mirrors back word for word by pausing the sender with a hand signal so that they can mirror accurately, meaning word for word. Mirroring word for word is more valuable than "being polite" and waiting until the end of the sentence. Send in statements that describe the situation in the way a camera would see it. A camera does not interpret or see intentions.

2) **Validation:** After the full send has been completed to the sender's satisfaction, the receiver validates the send by first summarizing what was said, *"In summary you're saying . . . Is this a good summary?"* Start by answering, *"Yes"*. Then, if the summary is not to the sender's satisfaction, the sender would say, *"And I'd like to clarify..., or I would like to underscore..."* The receiver Mirrors the corrections. Once the sender is satisfied with the receiver's summary, the receiver adds several validating sentences:

   - *"I listened carefully to what you said."*
   - *"Your perspective is important and valuable to me."* and
   - *"You make sense."*

3) **Empathy:** The receiver then guesses what the sender might be feeling now or might have felt in the past, saying something *like "Last night, you might have felt hurt and unimportant, but now you feel heard and respected. Is that what you're feeling?"* The sender then replies to the receiver's guess, saying perhaps *"Yes, I felt hurt and unimportant!"* The receiver would then inquire, *"Are there any more feelings you have about that?"*

The sender might then say, *"Yes, I also felt disconnected and scared,"* after which the receiver would empathize by saying *"You also felt disconnected and scared. All those feelings make sense to me. I can see how you felt/feel that way."*

4) **Response:** At this point the original receiver becomes the new sender and says, *"I would like to respond."* The original sender is now the new receiver and goes through the three steps of Mirroring, Validation, and Empathy. The Response must stay on topic. Giving a good Response takes practice. Being defensive or setting the record straight isn't constructive. Instead, it is important that the new sender first own what he can own (remember Pillar #4). This might sound like, *"I own that I arrived late for our date and did not give you a call."* The new receiver mirrors that back. The new sender might continue with, *"It makes sense to me that you felt overlooked and unimportant,"* the new receiver mirrors that back. The new sender then may say, *"I regret not having called you to let you know that I would be late,"* and the new receiver mirrors. A nice ending might be, *"I will make sure that I stay on top of that in the future,"* which again the receiver Mirrors. Finally, *"Thank you for bringing this up to me in such a straightforward and respectful way."*

Throughout this process, it is important that the new sender does not initially get defensive and try to explain why he was late. That would invalidate the original send. On the other hand, if both feel well grounded and emotionally strong, it could be appropriate to explain why he was late, not as an excuse or a defense, but as a piece of information respectfully given. One example of this would be to say, *"I feel so bad that my phone ran out of juice and I couldn't call you to let you know of the accident on the freeway."* That would go a long way toward helping the receiver get beyond her anger and believe that the sender simply forgot and didn't care. But there is no hard-and-fast rule as to the timing of any explanation. It may be OK to give an explanation in the current Dialogue, or it may be wiser done in a later Dialogue. Many of us have a strong urge to explain and defend ourselves, thus forgetting to "remain grounded in our innocence (Pillar #2)." Use your best judgment and practice the skills of attuned listening.

A Step-by-Step Guide to the Formal Dialogue
(What is spoken is printed in bold)

SENDER	RECEIVER
a. Make an appointment: **"I would like to have a Formal Dialogue. Is this a good time for you?"**	b. **"Yes, this is a good time."** or, **"No, not for now."** The sender should respect this.
Phase 1. Mirroring	
a. Make a short statement, which is called a send. **"I would like to talk about . . .**	b. Hold up a hand and Mirror the send, word for word. **" You would like to talk about . . .**
c. Keep on sending, in short statements.	d. Hold up a hand after each send and Mirror word for word. Continue to do this until the sender says, **"That's all."** If unsure, the receiver can ask, **"Is there anything more you would like to say about this?"**
Phase 2: Validation	
	a. Summarize all that the sender has said, saying, **"In summary, what you're saying is . . ."**
	b. Verify the accuracy of the summary by asking, **"Is that a good summary?"**
c. Always answer **"Yes."** The sender must be encouraging, so answers can be **"Yes, AND I would like to underscore…"** or **"Yes, AND I would like to clarify..."** Avoid saying **"Yes, but…"** since that negates the **"Yes."**	d. Continue to Mirror the Senders clarifications if there are any.
	e. Validate the sender by saying, **"I listened carefully to what you had to say. "Your perspective is important and valuable to me. "You make sense."** (NOTE: This does NOT mean "I agree with you.")

Phase 3: Empathy	
	a. Make one or two guesses about what the sender is feeling in this situation, saying, **"I imagine you might be feeling... (hurt and lonely). Is that what you're feeling?"**
b. Answer **"Yes**, (and then repeat the feelings) **I am feeling... (hurt and lonely)"** The repeating helps the sender clarify and own his or her feelings. Or they may say, **"No, I am feeling disconnected and abandoned."**	c. If the sender's answer is **"Yes,"** ask, **"Do you have any more feelings about this?"** Mirror the additional feelings. Now Mirror all the sender's true feelings.
	d. Once you have verified the sender's true feelings, say, **"All those feelings make sense to me. I can see how you feel/felt that way."**

Phase 4: Response	
	a) Say, **"I would like to respond."** At this point, you become the new sender and the original sender becomes the new receiver.
	b) Begin the response with a positive statement like, ' **"What I can own is . . ."** or **"What touched me about what you said is . . ."** Don't begin the response with a negative or critical statement like, **"Here's what I think about that..."** or **"You're wrong, I can't believe you said that."** Stay on the topic of the original sender. Giving your own perspective is changing the subject.

Repeat Phases 1, 2 and 3, with the new sender making statements and the new receiver Mirroring, Validating, and Empathizing with them, staying on the topic of the original sender. We recommend just one back and forth. Without a coach, limit the sends to 10 minutes.

(Giving your own perspective is changing the subject.)

Appendix 2

The Theory of Imago Relationship Therapy

Imago Relationship Therapy is a form of couples' therapy developed by Harville Hendrix and his wife, Helen LaKelly Hunt, in the mid 1980's. Their book, *Getting The Love You Want: A Guide for Couples*, became a New York Times best seller in 1988. Harville has been on the *Oprah Winfrey Show* seventeen times. Oprah calls him "The marriage whisperer," and "My favorite couples' therapist."

This phenomenon gave rise to an explosive interest in Imago Relationship Therapy and led to the development of the organization of Imago Relationships International.

The following is theoretical and may hold none or minimal interest for some of you. This is perfectly alright, and in no way would hinder your capacity to benefit from the practices we recommend in this trilogy.

IMAGO THEORY: SOME BASIC CONCEPTS

1. Healthy babies are born whole and complete. Our natural state as neonates is to feel alive – to experience empathic connection as well as a state of relaxed joyfulness, especially while in the arms of our mother.

2. We became wounded by our parents and other caregivers, usually inadvertently, during the early nurturing and socialization stages of our development – primarily the first three years. Our parents did their best and therefore do not deserve to be judged. Nevertheless, they made mistakes and we all suffered some degree of woundedness because of them. We lost our original wholeness, aliveness, and empathic connection.

3. We all yearn to heal our childhood wounds in order to restore our aliveness. We also yearn to grow into our full potential and become whole. All animals and plants have the same inner drive: to become the best they can be given the environmental conditions they find themselves in.

4. Because of these wounds, we developed patterns of defenses – protective mechanisms that we call our character structure – in order to keep us safe during childhood. These protective mechanisms include constricting and pulling back our energy (minimizing) or expanding and pushing forward our energy (maximizing). Some of the maximizing defenses include becoming a clinger or a pursuer, or being diffuse or manipulative. Some of the minimizing defenses involve becoming an isolating or distancing person, or sometimes becoming rigid or competitive.

5. Our experiences with our parents, from birth on, got imprinted in some primitive, nonverbal parts of our brain and our body. By the time we reach adulthood, we have a rich tapestry of those imprints (both positive and negative experiences). We call this inner, unconscious catalogue of our experiences with our parents and significant adults, the Imago. The Imago is an unconscious image of those experiences, imprinted at the deepest level of our being. This imprinting process exists in all mammals, and that includes us humans. It is in the service of survival, and

allows the young to know who their parents are and to rush to them for protection in times of danger.

6. This inner image, the Imago, is the unconscious roadmap that leads us to a person we will fall in love with—a person who does, symbolically, represent the negative aspects of both Mom and Dad all wrapped up into one. We call that person an "Imago Match". This Imago Match is just the right person with whom to finish our unfinished business and heal the wounds of our childhoods. Thus, the Imago theory postulates that the primary goal of committed, intimate relationships is healing and growth. A common destructive myth is that the goal of marriage is to be happy. What's beautiful, though, is that the by-product of growth and healing work will indeed, be happiness! We *can* reach the state of happiness we all yearn for.

7. As we were growing up, some characteristics in our parents hurt us. In the committed intimate relationship, we are now in the presence of a person who will awaken in us all those negative imprints – a person who will touch our raw nerves – but also a person who can now choose to love us the way we need to be loved and give us what our parents never could. Concurrently, we are called upon to reciprocate and become a healer for our partner. Ah! We feel safe with that person. We feel loved. We experience the healing and wholeness we had been yearning for.

8. Romantic Love is the door into a committed, intimate relationship (living together or marriage), and it is nature's way of connecting us with just the right person for our eventual healing and growth.

9. When we make *a full commitment* to this person, we enter the Power Struggle stage of relationships. The Power Struggle is essential, for embedded in a couple's frustrations lie the information for healing and growth. We have a saying in Imago:

"Conflict is growth trying to happen!" We often misinterpret conflict to mean that we are not right for each other. On the contrary, conflict provides the main impetus and opportunity for change and personal development.

10. We engage in the first two stages of couplehood – Romantic Love and the Power Struggle – at an unconscious level. Our unconscious mind chooses our partner for the purpose of healing childhood wounds. During the Romantic Love stage, we are reactively nice. During the Power Struggle stage, we are reactively unkind and critical.

11. We will discover, to our consternation, that upon making a full commitment (either in marriage or moving in together), our love partner is incompatible with us, least able to meet our needs, and most able to re-wound us all over again. This is because we are an Imago Match, meaning we are equally wounded but carry complementary energies (minimizers and maximizers couple up). Consequently, we struggle with the other's way of doing things. We are now between a rock and a hard place, and we will be forced to grow up or get out. When we discover this, we feel deeply disillusioned and betrayed, and we wonder if we are with the "wrong" person.

12. The goal of Imago Relationship Therapy is to assist clients to develop a conscious, intimate and committed relationship that becomes a crucible where healing and growth can happen.

13. The definition of healing is getting emotional needs met that were not met in childhood. For example, healing can be feeling acknowledged and appreciated instead of ignored and neglected.

14. The definition of growth is the modification of our character defenses. Character defenses (maximizing or minimizing) protected us from pain in childhood. Now those very same defenses that worked well for us as children, block us from having

closeness as adults. The modification of our defenses will allow us to grow into maturity.

15. The journey toward healing and growth moves us from reactivity (that which we do spontaneously) to intentionality (that which we decide to do to counter our reactivity).

16. All couples have the same diagnosis: Emotional Symbiosis. This is quite different from biological symbiosis, in which two organisms interact to their mutual advantage. Emotional Symbiosis in couples occurs when one partner wants the other to think, feel and believe just like he or she does: "I want you to see the world my way, and when you don't, I feel threatened." We are all on a journey of letting go of the idea that you need to think, feel and believe the way I do in order for me to love you.

    This transition from symbiosis to differentiation does not take place through insight. We must practice specific skills and processes often and regularly to shift us from having an unconscious relationship (reactive and symbiotic) to having a conscious relationship (intentional and differentiated). Healthy differentiation is what allows us to experience connection. If I can let you be you (differentiation), you will feel safe with me and therefore experience connection with me.

17. All couples desire passion. A non-negotiable condition for passion is safety. Therefore, Imago practice focuses on keeping each other safe in each other's presence.

    Couples want to be in touch with the life force they were born with. They want to feel the excitement that "you and I make a great team!" They want to feel effective and energized in the world. They want to feel sexually alive. Passion is a function of safety. As we do "the work" safety increases and passion emerges.

The safety we are trying to achieve is the safety to be ourselves without the fear of judgment or retaliation from our partner. In Imago, we believe that safety is achieved through the use of structure. The main structure we teach couples is embedded in Dialogues in various forms. The Formal Dialogue forces us to listen to each other, therefore slowly ushering in a greater disclosure of the self and a sense that indeed we are connected.

It often takes several years of regular work together to get to that place and achieve the relationship of your dreams

GETTING THE LOVE YOU WANT COUPLES WORKSHOP

We recommend that you attend a "Getting The Love You Want Couples Workshop" (which was designed by Harville Hendrix and his wife Helen LaKelly Hunt in the 70s and 80s) to get a full introduction to the various Dialogues and exercises.

When Harville got divorced in the early 70's, he was a professor of Marriage and Family at Southern Methodist University in Texas – and the irony of it hit him very hard. After he and Helen got married they dedicated their lives to figuring out why being an intimate couple in today's world is so difficult. Harville and Helen's 1988 New York Times Best-Selling book, *Getting the Love You Want: A Guide for Couples* came out of the workshops they had developed for couples over the previous decade. They saw the intimate couple as the foundation of society, and determined that the childhood wounding that results in all the ills of society starts in the home of origin. They came to the conclusion that the best way to heal society is to bring healing to intimate couples. The analogy they use is, "Stop the pollution upstream and then we won't need to spend all the billions of dollars trying to clean up the pollution downstream" - jails, child abuse, teen pregnancies, broken homes, robberies, murders, war and on and on.

The workshop has stood the test of time. Scores of these same workshops are put on every weekend all over the world by Certified Imago Workshop Presenters who have been trained at the Imago International Institute. As a result, there are several hundred thousand couples who have taken the workshop not only in the United States but in over thirty-five countries around the world.

The workshop is a seminar, NOT group therapy. You and your partner may remain as private as you choose. All the work is done between you as a couple. You get a comprehensive manual. There are lectures, demonstrations, workbook exercises, and periods of Dialogue with your partner using the processes that have just been modeled. Coaching is available throughout the two days. Couples often find this intensive workshop to have the same value as six months of couples counseling.

For more information, go to the website www.gettingtheloveyou-want.com

References

We referred to these books at various places in any of the three volumes.

Beauvoir, Francine. *Raising Cooperative and Self-Confident Children: A Step-by-step Guide for Conscious Parenting.* Pasadena Press, 1997

Frankl, Viktor. *Man's Search for Meaning.* Boston: Beacon Press, 2006

Hendrix, Harville. *Getting the Love You Want: A Guide for Couples.* New York: Holt, 1988/1998.

_____ *Keeping the Love You Find: A Guide for Singles.* New York: Pocket Books, 1992.

Kingma, Daphne Rose. *A Garland of Love: Daily Reflections on the Magic and Meaning of Love.* Berkeley, CA: Conari Press, 1992.

Kramer, Greg. *Insight Dialogue: The Interpersonal Path to Freedom.* Boston: Shambhala: 2007.

Lerner, Harriet Goldhor. *Marriage Rules: A Manual for the Married and the Coupled Up.* New York: Gotham Books, 2012.

Luquet, Wade. *Short-Term Couples Therapy: The Imago Model in Action.* New York: Routledge, 2007.

Mellody, Pia, Andrea Wells Miller, and Keith Miller. *Facing Codependence: What It Is, Where It Comes From, and How It Sabotages Our Lives.* San Francisco: Perennial, 1989.

Muller, Wayne, *Legacy of the Heart: The Spiritual Advantages of a Painful Childhood.* Simon and Schuster, 1993

Remen, Rachel Naomi, *Kitchen Table Wisdom.* Publishers Weekly. July 29, 1996

Rohr, Richard, *Hope Against Darkness: The Transforming Vision of Saint Francis.* St Anthony Messenger Press, 2001

Smedes, B. Lewis, *Forgive and Forget: Healing the Hurts We Don't Deserve.* Harper & Row, San Francisco, 1984

_____*The Art of Forgiving: When You Need to Forgive and Don't Know How.* Moorins, Nashville, 1996

Siegel, Daniel J. *The Mindful Therapist: A Clinician's Guide to Mindsight and Neural Integration.* W. W. Norton, New York, 2010

About the Authors

Francine Beauvoir, Ph.D, and Bruce Crapuchettes, Ph.D are both licensed psychologists, married to each other for fifty years and parents of four adult children. Over the past 20 years, they have run over ten weekend workshops per year worldwide for couples, parents and singles wanting to be in relationship. They have also run five couples groups and two groups for individuals continuously during that same period of time.

Francine received her Ph.D. from U.S.C. in Los Angeles and is the author of *"Raising Cooperative And Self-Confident Children: a step-by-step guide for conscious parenting."*

Bruce received his Ph.D. from Fuller Graduate School of Psychology in Pasadena. He was dean of the faculty of the Imago International Institute from 2003 to 2005.

Both are members of the American Psychological Association, of Imago Relationships International and are on the faculty of the Imago International Institute. They co-founded the Pasadena Institute For Relationships in 1990, where they trained licensed psychotherapists in the specialty of Imago Relationship Therapy until 2014.

They can be reached by writing to:
bruce@pasadenainstitute.com or francine@pasadenainstitute.com
See also: www.pasadenainstitute.com

Bruce and Francine

Made in the USA
San Bernardino, CA
01 March 2018